BLUES GUITAR
INSIDE & OUT

WRITTEN AND
ILLUSTRATED
BY
RICHARD DANIELS

This book was produced in good faith, and with full respect for the legacy of American blues music and all of the people that are a part of it. All layout, page design, ink drawings and technical diagrams were provided by the author.

All typesetting was done by Horizon Printing and Graphics, Newark, Delaware, so, thanks to Barbara for the long haul. Some of the pictures, and all of the darkroom work were meticulously produced by Corky Becker. A million thanks to Betsy, and also Jesse, for all of their help. Thanks also go out to Mike, and all of my railroad friends in New Castle County, Delaware. And thanks again to Lauren and Company at Cherry Lane for once more making it happen.

Blues Guitar - Inside and Out was independently produced by The Heavy Guitar Company, Great Falls, VA 22066

Cherry Lane Music Co., inc.

"quality in printed music"

P.O. BOX 430 • PORT CHESTER, NY 10573

Table of Contents

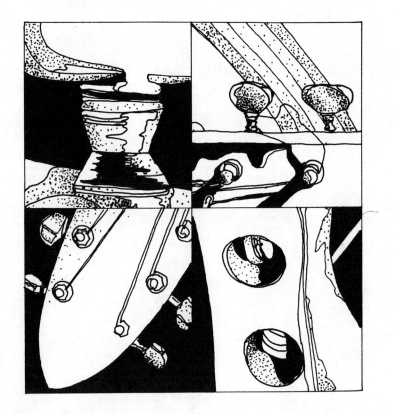

1. They Meet On Tracks

The harmonies of the early morning gospel show quietly drift across the small room. The street scene outside the open window begins to beat with the pulse of a city at dawn. A boy sits on the edge of the sill gazing out to the horizon, counting to himself the city blocks until a mist finally blurs the smallest image. His guitar sits quietly on his lap as he holds the neck and gently lifts the fretboard up to his eyes. Something comes over him as he looks closely at the grain of the guitar's wood. In the new morning light it becomes apparent how the overall systems of the guitar work. His eye sweeps over the body like a hawk gliding over an open field, pushing in close on each feature. The six strings, each with its own diameter, tension and placement, seem to have great purpose. What he had glazed over before didn't seem simple anymore.

He drinks in his own realizations one by one. The invention of the fret to shorten the vibrating string, the calculated distance between the strings, the construction of the acoustic sound box to both hold the strings and project their movement . . . nothing seems random. It becomes evident that all of the guitar's dimensions have been determined by the reach of the human hand, the hand of a musician from another generation.

Realizing he had drifted off, he took a deep breath, held the guitar straight and strummed an open chord. "Systems active," he laughed out into the room over the sound of the ringing strings. He wondered why he had never seen the guitar in this light before. He couldn't distinguish exactly why he had this sudden flash of understanding, but he felt the moment some sort of turning point. Things had been building up inside the boy for quite a while. Playing guitar had unconsciously become his first choice of how to spend time. No matter what else happened in the boy's life, when he was alone without obligation to the outside, he would pick up the guitar and strum. His discoveries came with a new sense of power. A growing confidence from knowing what he wanted drove him on. With a clearer sense of purpose, a sobering question settled in on him like a red light. How was he going to learn how to play the way he wanted?

He would hear the guitars on the radio, television and records and wanted to know more about actually putting it down when it came to fingers and strings. He instinctively felt the beat from the song's essence. Whole songs played in his mind as if the record was spinning on the turntable. He felt the sentiment of the music in his blood, but when it came time to play it on his own, it often went cold. He was frustrated by his lack of fretboard knowledge . . . all he had was the feeling.

The guitar lessons had come and gone along with the hope for understanding the sounds that he wanted to make. Each teacher was limited because of the linear style he taught — read dots, play "Red River Valley," and strum the chord. What did that have to do with the sounds he heard? The blues licks that jump off the record, those jazzy sounding chords, that rock and roll rhythm . . . all the teachers were removed from this part of the music world. They never listened to the boy's honest demand to learn that fast moving blues guitar.

The blues songs from his father's old record collection were his favorite. He would sing along with the whole side of an album again and again. He was constantly exposed to all types of popular music through his friends, many of whom played the guitar. The same thing kept happening whenever he would ask another guitar friend to play and push forward on the instrument. They would jam, but the others were satisfied to fake through the songs. It just didn't sound right. A lot of guys were content to put the guitar on the same level as the movies or just driving around, but he wanted to find out the truth about how the music was played, not just pass over it lightly.

The music of the guitar provided the boy with a wonderful, new, private world. The magnet of real world worries pulled everybody else onto an uninteresting treadmill. But to the boy, the sounds of the guitar stood as natural as the sun in the sky, an image of the most natural concern.

Standing up and moving for his coat, he suddenly found himself restless to move out onto the streets. He grabbed his guitar with the palm of his hand carefully muting the strings. With his coat buttoned and the guitar protectively held in front of him, he weaved his way out of his parents' living room, down the old wood steps to the heavy glass door, then out onto the open sidewalk.

The chemistry of the fresh air made his senses pound with a new-found freedom. There was a nip in the morning air, but the warm sensation he felt kept him immune from the elements. He didn't give much thought to where he was walking or even why. He just followed himself out of the house and away. With the guitar over his shoulder and out of harm's way, the street offered itself up to him. Everybody went forcefully ahead to jobs without question, and the boy felt his place was with the guitar as he walked among the crowd.

People would look twice at the boy's determined figure as he walked past the blocks of stores, theatres, banks and offices. On and on he pushed until he could see the outskirts of the industrial district. Preoccupied with the distant horizon leading out of town, the present mile was only to be walked over — nothing more. It was where he was going that was important. Music reigned his thoughts as the factory trucks and wire link fence flowed by like water under a riverboat. Nothing determined his course as he clutched the guitar's neck and suddenly ran up a steep embankment onto the railroad tracks.

Leaving behind the cars, trucks and buildings on the street, he entered into the world of the rails. He kept his eyes down as he stepped up onto the elevated roadbed, walking the ties, watching for large cinders that sometimes worked themselves up onto the wood. He was almost afraid to look up, because he knew how far the tracks stretched. It was too far to understand. "Never walked these rails before," he said out loud. Looking up, he gazed down the tracks to where they seemingly came together and he drew in a sharp breath.

He felt a great affinity for the world of the rails as he walked by the old railway bridges and station yards. Everything was vastly overdesigned to accomodate the huge diesel locomotives. The tracks seemed like a place where nobody would ever bother him — a place where time just passed on. There was a built-in sense of loneliness — not a place where you stay, but a scene where you keep moving on. He felt a respect for the men that lay the rails, and those that continue the thankless job of running the trains back and forth across the same miles.

He tuned his guitar as he continued to walk. As the miles went by, he pounded out the chords to a few old songs. Pacing the distance between the ties became second nature to the boy as the song melodies melted into the air. He felt like a drop of water in a bucket. Now he could sing without being ashamed and strum to the steel in the rails. The rails remained the same.

If a certain song seemed right, he would sing it again and again, each time getting stronger. Gone was the anxiety he felt in his room for finding a way to learn. It no longer bothered him. He was committed to his new-found energy. Hours passed and the noon sun burned the fields that surrounded the tracks. He played every song — even the early ones that he learned but had forgotten were once again rolled out.

Stopping on a switchplate, the boy looked up from his guitar to see that the city had disappeared behind him into a gray haze too faint to recognize. Everything around him dazzled green with growth. The sparse farm buildings of weathered wood could be seen in expansive fields. He decided to follow the side track which went into a sweeping bend towards a thick woods. As the main tracks slowly curved out of sight, he wondered to himself where the side tracks would take him. He decided on a trestle bridge a quarter mile ahead as a good resting point. As the sun beat down on his arms and back, he thought maybe this was far enough out, alone with the guitar.

He set his pace for the bridge, looking out in the woods to get a bearing on the distance and size of the trees which grew along the rails. Suddenly he stopped, bringing both feet to rest on a single wooden tie. Muting the guitar's strings with the flesh of his hand, he stood like a stone statue with his eyes in a tight squint and his breath held silent. What was it that he heard? It was so faint that he had to focus all of his attention to his hearing. He sensed a blend of breeze across the woods and some kind of sweet music. It seemed so steady, so perfectly in tune that the boy did not notice his own gradual movement towards the source. Each step towards the bridge brought the music in clearer until the boy knew that what he heard was a single guitar. There was no doubt — it was the blues being played as never before! The rolling notes were mesmerizing, filled with a mysterious energy. The boy shook his head to the sky. What was it doing out here ... another guitar?

As the force of the music grew each moment, an outline of a man with a guitar began to take shape as the bridge came into full view. After hours of solitude, the events of the day quickly flashed through his stimulated mind. What brought him to this place? Why did he feel so full of wonderous energy? Why did the music he heard affect him so strongly?

As the boy approached the bridge, he could see that the lone guitar player was an old man with weathered skin. As the music drew the boy in for a closer look, the old man acknowledged the boy's presence by simply looking down and pushing further into his song. They both quietly stared down at the body of the singing guitar. As the minutes drifted by, the strings rang out the melancholy message of the blues. The blues beat seemed all around. The old man played with a sincere conviction that overwhelmed the young boy. Without a word being spoken, the boy knew that this was his one chance to get a first-hand look at the music he had heard but could never figure out.

Without missing a beat, the old man looked up into the boy's eyes and said, "What is it, Boy?"

The boy gazed down at the rails. "Can you teach me how to play like that?"

The old man sat up straight on his railroad tie. "Well now, the answer to your question is yes, but only if you are ready to listen, to concentrate, and to practice — that will determine if you learn or not."

The boy took two steps back. His dreams were coming true. He had to immediately sharpen his wits. "Yes, I am ready to study."

Nodding slowly, the old man replied, "Good, because my time is precious, and you should never take it for granted. The day will come when you know well what I have to offer, and the train will take me to another...but if you say that you are ready, I will call up my power to teach you."

With this the boy knew that he had crossed the invisible line into a new world. Everything that had happened to him in the course of this strange day now took on a baffling overall pattern. Things were moving too fast to figure out what forces were actually at work. He was simply grateful for the privilege of meeting this puzzling old man who immediately seemed to take the boy's best interest to heart. The shear conviction with which the old man played was the element missing from the world that he had left behind in the city.

"Now, I'll teach you the first rule of the rails. When the train comes, get off the tracks." The boy frowned with a look of puzzlement. Silently, the old man pointed to where the rails went to the horizon and said, "Listen!" The boy heard nothing at first, but after a few moments of held silence, the faintest sounds could be discerned, and the boy's brow went smooth.

"How could you have heard that train a full minute ago, Old Man?"

"Why, that is only amazing to you because you didn't hear it. I hear what I hear."

"Come on and follow me, Boy." They picked up their guitars and the boy followed the old man along a dirt utility road that ran parallel to the tracks in the direction of the oncoming train. "You have gone through the 'quiet time' already, Boy. This is the time when you stand still and let your mind hear that distant train. This will be like your quiet study lesson. The 'loud time' is guitar party — when everything is moving fast and your guitar is flashing out the riffs that make the high times happen. It's all part of the range of things you have to do. Don't forget: it's 'quiet time' first, then 'loud'."

The rumble of the train grew increasingly louder as the old man stood tall and braced himself. "Now take a few deep breaths and steady yourself for the engine's passing, for it is stronger than you know."

The boy pumped fresh air through his nose which heightened his senses. The train seemed to block the sky as it approached with a steely wall of sound. The boy widened his stance and closed his eyes as the engine's power overcame his senses. Experiencing the whirlwind of the moment, the boy deciphered a strange primal cry mixed with the locomotive's roar. Opening his eyes, he saw the old man standing with his arms outstretched to the movement of the train, howling at the top of his lungs at the superhuman momentum created by the steel wheels. The boy was beside himself as he drank in the spectacle. The glint in the old man's eye showed the boy once and for all that the old man had a fierce drive for experiencing the truth of the moment, drawing on a tremendous reserve of energy.

The caboose finally ripped by and left the boy in a whirl rubbing his eyes. By the time the boy had cleared his head, the old man was already walking between the rails. "Jump up on the rails while they're still hot!" The boy approached the area above the rail with great reserve, slowly reaching down to examine the rail's surface.

"Don't feel too hot."

"No, but maybe the sun will heat them up after a while. Besides, you know a little bit more about the rails now that you've had a closer look.

"Walk up beside me for a while Boy, and I'll tell you some stories about the way things came to be. Now, you were playing guitar earlier on the rails, you know some songs, and you have lived through the recent age of rock guitar. But, did you ever get the feeling that you were missing something from the whole picture? Are you aware of the musical heritage that has gone before you, and are free to draw upon however you wish? The history of the blues is an American tale in which you can find your place even now. You have to go back to the old records and hear the voices of the past tell you their own story. Along with the music, you will feel the missing space in time between you and the musician, and you will sense their particular situation. Their whole world will open up to you. One thing is for sure: they knew nothing of modern times. You will hear this when they sing and play.

"How far should I take you back, Boy? Do you know about the African heritage? Imagine thousands of years of drums pounding out the lifeblood pulse of the steamy, ruthless jungle. The dark droning voices, the intense frantic dancing, the simultaneous polyrhythms created by scores of fast moving drums — this was part of the tribes' communal life. The most important function of the

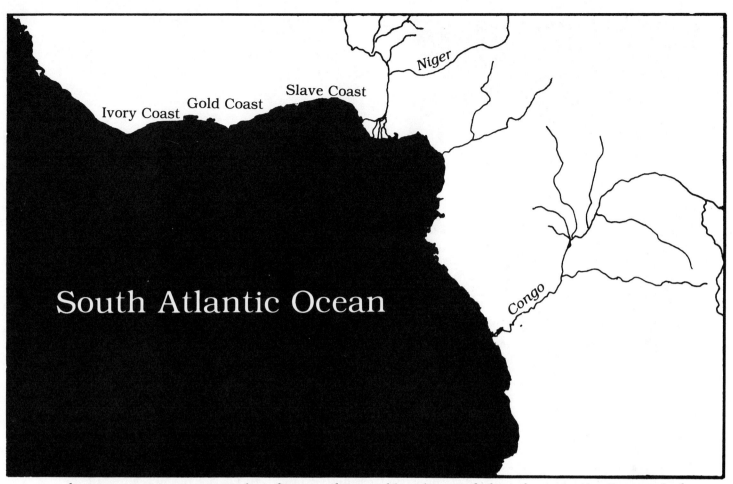

drums was not enjoyment, but the way they could make you feel — sharp, instinctive, ready for action. It may not have been understood as music at all, but something that was necessary to survive the fierce environment of the earth's equatorial region.

"Importation of Africans to American shores began in 1619 when a Dutch frigate in distress landed in Jamestown, Virginia, and exchanged twenty African slaves for food and supplies. This started a slave trade that lasted over two centuries and determined the course of history in the American South. The slaves themselves represented a wide array of ethnic and linguistic groups including the Wolof, Malinke, Fulani, Akan, Yorruba, Ibo and Kongo. Approximately 400,000 slaves were brought to the United States during the period 1619-1865, but because of breeding, the overall number grew to approximately 3,000,000 by the beginning of the Civil War in 1860. In order to really see the picture, you should also know that for every slave brought to America, there were seven taken to Brazil, and eight to the Carribean Islands.

"Slaves were taken in great numbers to the Georgia Sea Islands which run from Charleston, South Carolina, down to Savannah, Georgia. The sailing ships that went through the Florida Keys took many slaves to New Orleans where they were then taken by smaller boats up the winding Mississippi River to plantations along the banks. Named the 'Father of Waters' by the Indians, the Mississippi played a great part in the shaping of the young country's destiny. It is considered to be the greatest of all American rivers. The Mississippi flows through nineteen states before it reaches New Orleans and the Gulf of Mexico. Its longest watercourse is 2550 miles and it has 100,000 tributaries that allow for 15,700 miles of inland navigation. The slave plantations flourished along the lowland banks for hundreds of miles above New Orleans because it was discovered that the river had deposited fertile soil in this area. The river's diversified network of waterways provided pioneers and traders with an excellent transportation system into the mainland from the Gulf. Little is known about what the real lives of the slaves were all about,because they had no legal rights and few records were kept. We are talking about 250 years of history — fifteen full generations of a people. Exclusive of the fact that they were made slaves by an outside unknown group of people, it is important to remember that these were real people. They had hopes, fears and feelings just as strong as you or I.

"The Mississippi black code was that slaves could not play drums or horns because owners were fearful that they would be used for communications to incite insurrection. But that didn't stop them from singing. The field workers would chant the hours away using a 'call and response' vocal method in which the lead worker would shout his message and the workers would repeat his call in unison. On some plantations, Sunday services were allowed and the old wooden floors would sway with the slow gospel beat — later carried over in the Negro Pentacostal Church. The memory of their heritage produced African elements in their tool design, tombstones and their music.

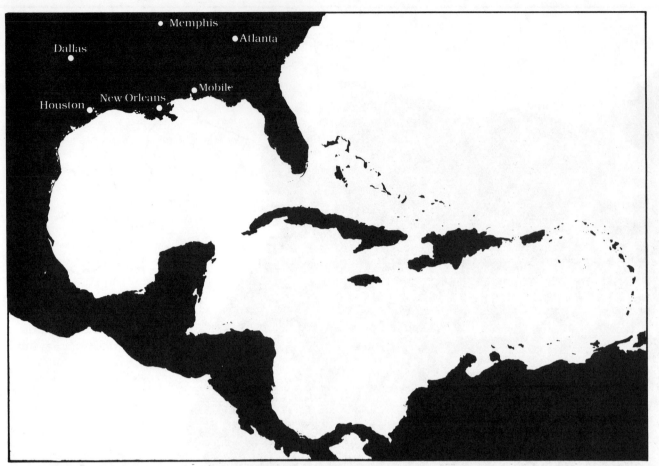

"In 1839, Fannie Anne Kemble, an English actress married to a Georgia rice planter, wrote in her *Journal of a Residence on a Georgia Plantation* about the force with which the slaves would sing during their work and play. The slaves were allowed to sing, but often the true message of the songs, usually of resentment or strife, had to be cleverly hidden by double meaning.

"Many of the plantation owners would permit the workers to have their good time party on Saturday night because they feared that without some sort of release, emotions would explode into trouble. The sun would go down, the songs would start, and the clapping and dancing would begin. Frolics, jigs, hollers, devil songs, over and over drags, stomps — call them what you will, they were the first blues parties. The workers cried about their condition, even if they were outwardly laughing with the good times. They were serious about their music. Many of the themes were about death and the endless wheel of work to which they were tied. Better singers knew that it was their time to perform, because that special night was for the raising of the spirit. They sang and yelled and went on until they were tired. Somehow that was enough.

"The end of the Civil War and freedom from slavery came in 1865, and as much of a milestone as this was, there was still a tremendous amount of suffering and oppression. You don't change minds with laws, and as the plantations broke down into smaller sharecrop farms, it was no secret who was in control when it came time to cash in the crop. A decade after the war, the government's 'Reconstruction Plan' failed and in 1877, the federal enforcement troops pulled out of the Louisiana State House. Many Negroes died as they tried to exercise their new 'legal' freedom, only to see one southern state after another pass laws that once again deprived them of their legal rights. There was an awful national depression in the 1890's that crushed the hope for a decent life. The boll weevil destroyed the cotton crops and the workers stood by as their crops were plowed under to protect the price of already harvested stock.

"Through it all, you have to see that there was a certain kind of development of character and forging of identity for the Negro. Many moved North with new-founded hope. The Negro Pentacostal Church thrived and the tradition of spiritual singing reached new heights. The banjo, originally from Africa, and the fiddle, brought by Irish and Scottish immigrants, came into widespread use in the South along with the mandolin and guitar. In the 1890's, American guitars became available from both the Orville Gibson and C. F. Martin guitar companies.

"Before the Civil War, the white commercial songwriters widely emulated the black elements. But after the war, the greatest influence was of white music on black. The black songwriter, James Bland, wrote *Carry Me Back To Old Virginny*, which is now the state song of Virginia. The field song tradition was carried on into the turn of the century by the field workers, the gangs in the southern penitentiaries and the laborers who worked laying the endless steel rails. Roustabout adventure and river lore 'levee' songs were popular in the 1880's. Songs were used as an easy way to tell a personal story, and were often full of small sayings, local color and idiosyncrasies of the performer. Song themes mirrored the hard times that the end of the century brought down on white and black alike. The population of Chicago increased tenfold between 1850 and 1900, and the militant *Chicago Defender* urged the Negro to 'quit' the south.

"Before we go any further and look at some individual blues people, let me remind you that blues origins were from country folk who were not necessarily outgoing memorable performers. I say this so you will remember that the names which do stick out are only a few of those that were really part of the whole movement.

"The first type of Negro-influenced music to really gain wide popularity was ragtime piano. Emerging at the end of the 1890's, this fast-moving piano music was painstakingly written for a single performer. It used three or four sections containing sixteen measures with a syncopated melody on a steady double beat. In 1899, Scott Joplin, a black piano man, published *Maple Leaf Rag,* which established him as the King of Ragtime Piano. St. Louis was the ragtime center where you could find such greats as Tom Turpin and Louis Chauvin taking ragtime to the World's Fair. 'Rags,' as the songs were called, were very difficult to perform because the right hand was called on to continually syncopate the melody, with the left hand playing a heavily accented 2°4 beat derived from military march music. Joplin wrote his music to be played at a slow tempo, but after a few years, many piano players picked up the speed in order to show off their dexterity.

"Now imagine that it's 1903 and we're sitting in the audience of a small theatre in Clarksdale, Mississippi, watching the Knights of Pythias Band and Orchestra, nine men in uniform, playing popular Broadway hits. After an hour or so of conventional performance, there is a call from the audience to play it loose. A local guitarist and bass fiddle player join the band on stage and the newcomers break into a down home 'over and over' which starts everybody tapping their feet. The feeling is contagious as the rest of the band and the crowd pick up on these guys who are stepping out. After a few times through, one of the band members steps to the front and improvises a free instrumental 'break' not written into the music. Other instruments follow suit and the crowd, excited by the loose form, applaudes for more. W. C. Handy is the band leader.

"Born in Florence, Alabama in 1873, W. C. Handy started a musical career in his youth that would last every day of his life and would change the course of popular American music. Handy is best known for his melodic blues songs, most of which were written and widely performed between 1910 and 1915. As a teenager, he was discouraged from being a musician by his Methodist minister father. After performing as a tenor in the town quartet, he put together another quartet and headed north to the Chicago World's Fair only to find the Fair cancelled. After this, he moved on through a number of musical groups from St. Louis to Indiana to Kentucky. He lived the flamboyant life of a traveling musician in the famous *Mahara's Colored Minstrel Show* between 1896 and 1903. He was a bandmaster and lead cornet player for the group which played medleys of old favorites like *Golden Slippers* and *Dixie*. But it was from his teaching of the *Memphis Colored Pythian Band* in 1905 that he started to pick up the members for his own band which played on Beale Street.

"In 1909, there were three prominent bands in Memphis: Eckford's, Bynum's and Handy's. The same year there was a three-way race for mayor in the city and each candidate employed one of the leading bands to advertise their campaign. Handy's band was hired by candidate E. H. Crump, and several sub-bands had to be organized in order to cover the entire voting district. Always ready with something new and innovative, Handy drew on the blues form and composed a song off-the-cuff called, what else, *Mr. Crump*. After laying it down for the band, Handy took his song out onto the corner of Main and Madison and within a few minutes, the crowd was dancing in the street. Needless to say, Crump won the election hands down, and the Handy band was in great demand for all sorts of performances. Handy was not only a great songwriter and performer, but after his reputation grew, he came to own a chain of bands that sent more than sixty different musicians out into the Memphis area on any given night. After several legal hassles, the song *Mr. Crump* was published in 1912 under its new title — *The Memphis Blues.*

"Handy had the uncanny ability to file away small incidents in his mind and then, years later, recall them perfectly for his immediate musical benefit. In 1914 he published *The St. Louis Blues* about his experiences there more than a decade before. In 1914 *The Yellow Dog Blues* was also published, and was based on a happenstance meeting in 1903 between Handy and an unknown guitarist in a Mississippi railway station. The loner was playing the strings with a knife blade and singing the same line three times about going to 'where the Southern crosses the Yellow Dog' — that's in Moorehead, Mississippi where the Yazoo Delta Railroad crosses the Southern Railroad. *The Hesitating Blues* and *Joe Turner* came out in 1915, then *Beale Street Blues* in 1916. These songs set a precedent for the use of the word 'blues' in a song title.

"Today it may not seem like any big deal that a guy published a few songs. But you have to understand the great influence that Handy's songs had on a lot of other bands that stopped in Memphis on their way up or down the river. Many other performers would include Handy's numbers on their national tours. The words to some of the songs did not fill up the entire space to the end of the bar, and this left an ideal place for the musician to improvise a little, or for the singer to yell out encouragement. The traveling bands found this form with the built-in space and the pure flowing melody lines to be a perfect medium to jazz up a 'hot' chorus. A loose counterpoint was used which simultaneously played one melodic line against another to produce a lively, dizzying effect. Of course, these were the elements of jazz. Down in New Orleans, Jelly Roll Morton was pounding the keys and incorporating all sorts of cosmopolitan influences into his rocking piano style. The Brown Brothers and the Original Dixieland Jazz Band were leaving the amusement halls smoking with the crowd yelling for more. In 1917, upon the insistance of the U.S. Navy, the red light district of the city known as Storyland was closed down. This deeply affected the musicians, many of which took a riverboat to points north.

"There are many pieces to the blues picture. The popularized blues of Handy were embraced in urban centers and influenced jazz development among the ensemble bands. It was the area of the Mississippi delta, however, that produced the 'one man, one guitar' idiom that comprised the country blues. When you hear people talk about the delta region, they don't mean down by New Orleans, although that area is certainly the final delta. You will see it marked that way on maps. The delta blues region is about 350 miles upriver from New Orleans and lies in an immense fertile lowland between Vicksburg and Memphis, with the Mississippi River to the west and the Yazoo River to the east. Almost in the shape of a D, the delta also known as the Mississippi alluvial plain, was the site of many early cotton plantations. Here the wide open vistas and the all-day dirt roads let you feel the silent power of the Mississippi as it meanders steadily through countless twists and turns along its thousand mile journey. All that a person can do is resign himself to the superhuman scale, and know that the rest of the picture is far off in some other part of America.

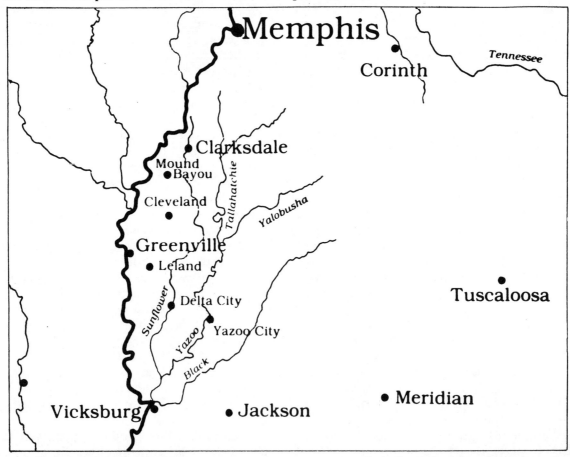

"Charlie Patton was the father and one of the best known of all the delta blues guitarists because of his aggressive vocals, derived from the field holler, and his straight on-the-beat percussive guitar work. Born one of twelve children in Edwards, Mississippi, he lived on Dockery's plantation near Cleveland, another delta town, until he was 34 years old. Early in Patton's development, he was influenced by an older musician named Henry Sloan. But it was on Dockery's plantation that he played with Tommy Johnson, Willie Brown, and dozens of others. The delta blues had a more personal, direct statement than the urban blues of the Handy tradition. The drone tonic low E string, the flatted third, the sliding and sluring of the voice over the broken rhythms, the quick vocal asides, and the dark brooding mood of the slow drag were all part of the blend that made up his style. The mold was forged directly from the musical elements of the fifty previous years into a heritage to be carried for generations to come. Even though Patton was an established blues singer by 1910, it wasn't until 1929 that he recorded his *Pony Blues* for Paramount. During the next five years Patton recorded almost seventy sides. Signed with the same company and good running friends of Patton were Tommy Johnson, acclaimed throughout the delta for his high falsetto, and Nehemiah 'Skip' James, who wrote the standard *I'm So Glad.*

"Inseparable from the music were the places where it was performed. Of course each guy had to do his homework to figure out the moves, but once those back road parties got started, it was a cycle that went until completion. Patton and all of the delta blues players were in demand throughout Mississippi for performance in dance halls, honky tonks, fish fries, gambling houses and, of course, at the parties put on by the musicians themselves.

"In 1926, a twenty-four year old guitarist by the name of Son House, blew into the delta from Louisiana. Highway 61 goes straight through the heart of the delta floodland and there are crossroads in the small towns of Indianola, Cleveland, Merigold and Shelby. The juke joints popped up at almost every stop in those days and Son House, equipped with his strong dark voice, his six string and slide, and his innate sense of timing was ready to take on — or at least entertain — all who came through the door for a drink. It wasn't long before Patton and House were comrades with Patton arranging for House's recording debut in 1930. Son House is known for *My Black Mama* and *Preaching The Blues* and sometimes sang with no musical accompaniment. He was younger than Patton and felt obliged to fill in the gap when his friend died in 1934. Son House recorded only twice. The first time was when he went to Grafton, Wisconsin, in 1930 with Charlie Patton to record for Paramount. The second recording was with Alan Lomax in 1942 when he was 42 years old and living in Robinsonville, Mississippi. So, when you hear him on record, it's from one of these two times.

"As history would have it, Son House would be remembered for more than just his performance. He greatly inspired a young man by the name of Robert Johnson, who would carry the torch of blues guitar tradition on into the thirties. We'll come back to Robert Johnson and the delta and pick this up in a minute. But, as I said before, Boy, there are many pieces to the blues picture.

"The word vaudeville is the corruption of the French 'Vau de Vire,' a locality in Normandy where popular songs were written in the 15th century — and was a name given to a type of variety show which became popular in the United States in the 1890's and flourished until the 1930's. Despite the image of a lonely man with a guitar singing his troubles away, the blues has always been a music with which to entertain. It is a very emotionally moving medium when the performer has the skill to pull it off. The blues is a line and the voice is the primary way to lay it down. Once the blues form was accepted as viable and embraced by entertainers, the vaudeville stage was a natural place for the music to get out to the crowds that loved it. Vaudeville was a very complex system of national stages, and there was a certain strata involved in what acts would appear in what theatres. A few of the circuits that would take on large scale shows were the Keith, Orpheum, and Pantages. Generally, they were racially segregated either by seating, show or day of the week.

"Many blues singers started out in circus acts with outfits such as the *Mighty Haag Circus.* The minstrel shows were smaller, but they were also widely accepted in the smaller towns where the bigger shows wouldn't venture. The most famous of all the minstrel shows was the *Rabbit Foot Minstrels.* Born in 1889, the much loved Ida Cox, who sang in only one key, worked with Rabbit Foot for many years, as did Ma Rainey, who set the pattern for those who followed. Ma Rainey toured widely in the south and was always welcome in town to sing her rendition of *Counting The Blues* with the lights gleaming off her necklace of twenty dollar gold pieces and the oversized eagle backdrop.

"Ten years younger than Ma Rainey was her heir, the incomparable Bessie Smith. Bessie forged the style known as the 'classic blues,' a hybrid jazz-blues singing approach which was used not only for strict blues numbers, but also to bring blues elements to standard ballads, ragtime and traditional songs.

"As rough as these tent shows were, they gave many blues performers a much-needed place to work. Walter 'Furry' Lewis, a Memphis singer guitarist, started out in a medicine show where health tonic was hawked outside the tent while he was singing songs like *John Henry.*

"There were five classic blues singers that used the name of Smith: Bessie, Trixie, Laura, Mamie and Clara. Mamie was working the *Orient* in Harlem when, in 1920, she opened the door for other blues singers with her best-selling *Crazy Blues.* The real potential of the classic blues singer was exemplified by Bessie Smith's 1923 recording of *Down Hearted Blues.* Trixie Smith was famous for her *Railroad Blues* and in 1922 won a blues singing contest in New York. Lillian Glinn from Texas and Hattie McDaniel, better known for her portrayal as Aunt Jemima, were also popular blues singers.

"After vaudeville's segregated circuit was functional for a few decades, the need for a Negro chain of theatres was satisfied by the opening of the *Theatre Owners Booking Agency* which flourished in the twenties. Although the conditions were tough and the pay was low, the T.O.B.A. or 'Toby Time,' as it came to be known, provided a real proving ground for hundreds of blues singers and musicians. Once you got on the bill, you could play the whole circuit of over forty cities: *The Pastime* on Beale Street in Memphis, *The Lyric* in New Orleans, *The Dream* in Columbus, and *The Park* in Dallas. Well, the Great Depression closed practically the whole scene down. But I'm telling you, Boy, those were the days.

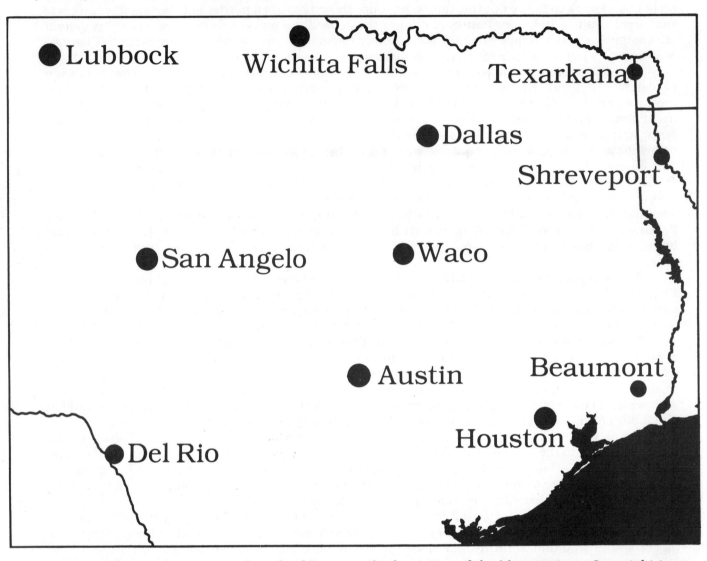

"Don't ever underestimate the role of Texas in the formation of the blues picture. One night in 1917, Walter Boyd, better known as Leadbelly, put a bullet into a man in a disagreement over a friend's girl while he was crossing a river in Texas near the Oklahoma state line. He ended up in the Texas pen with a sentence of thirty years hard labor. The legend goes that when Texas governor, Pat Neff, visited the prison a few years later, Leadbelly picked up his old twelve string guitar and demanded the man's attention by singing, 'If I had the Gov'ner where the Gov'ner has me, before daylight I'd set the gov'ner free.' Well, it might not have been before morning, but a parole came through in January, 1925.

"Way before this happened, Leadbelly made himself a name throughout Texas as a folk guitarist of the old 'songster' tradition. This was a mixture of old west ballads, ox and driver songs, cowboy tunes and western hard-time blues. He called himself 'the king of the twelve string guitar players of the world,' but you have to hear his voice to really understand. Blind Lemon Jefferson was the biggest influence on Leadbelly, and it's been said that they used to run through Dallas bars together just living the life. Blind Lemon used an arpeggio guitar style, along with his singing derived from the 'field holler,' and built himself a huge following as he traveled tirelessly throughout the south.

"The feeling from the Texas guitarists was a little more open and swinging than the insistent percussive techniques of the delta bluesmen. Blind Lemon made great use of a wide variety of techniques such as repeated hammer, slurring, and choking the string at the fret. He was also known to suspend the rhythm — that is just stop playing — when he went to sing. Talk about effective, that's it!

"Down on the rails near Elm Street in Dallas where the Central Line came through, you could hear Blind Lemon, Rambling Thomas, or Texas Alexander. Yeah, they would just play for each other rather than not at all. This is how the blues grew up. Down in the 'Froggy Bottom' section of the city where the hard country life spawned one juke or 'chock' house after another, and cheap whiskey flowed for small change, a barrel house piano player named Alexander Moore was putting down the full tilt scattered type of blues piano style that developed into Texas boogie-woogie and eventually into rhythm and blues. Shreveport, Louisiana was a stepping stone to the eastern cities and was a frequent stop for many musicians.

"Of course, we have to talk about things one at a time, but that's not really the way that it happened. Once she got rolling, many things happened at the same time, over a long period of time. Over in Atlanta, Peg Leg Howell was playing *The Broke and Hungry Blues* in the streets while Barbeque Bob helped establish a regional style with his percussive twelve string playing. Tampa Red, 'The Guitar Wizard,' was working with hokum bands which combined humor and good times with kazoos, guitars and mandolins all in a blues based format. He went up to Chicago after a while and became a big recording artist.

"Now up in St. Louis, a fine blues singer by the name of Peetie Wheatstraw was widely recorded in the thirties. His often-copied trademark was to use a delicate falsetto for the last measure of the singing. St. Louis was a big piano town in the thirties when Roosevelt Sykes came out with his piano hit *44 Blues.* In Indianapolis, the piano-guitar team of Leroy Carr and Scrapper Blackwell recorded over 100 sides between 1928 and 1935. Carr delivered the piano with an unusual understated vocal delivery while Blackwell's six-string Dobro technique combined delicate vibrato with the sound of the finger being snapped off the string.

"Jug bands were also popular, with their guitars, banjos, harmonicas, jugs, washboards, upright bass — you name it. Those guys who played the jug could only really play two or three notes, but the secret was to consistantly provide a bass note on the beat. That's how they worked. The Memphis Jug Band recorded *Bottle It Up and Go* in 1932, and The Cannon Jug Stompers became famous for their 1929 recording of *Walk Right In.* The Mississippi Sheiks was a three-man group consisting of singer-guitarist Walter Vinson, fiddler Lonnie Chatmon, and guitarist Bo Carter. They played mostly for white square dances and produced a huge hit in 1930 with *Sittin' On Top of the World.* Blind Willie McTell, Curley Weaver and Fred McMullen, Frank Stokes, Blind Blake, Memphis Minnie, Sleepy John Estes, Mississippi John Hurt — all of these blues artists recorded in the late twenties or early thirties, and they all loved the blues.

"The jazz tradition also flourished in the twenties, and Chicago proved to be a magnet for most of the musicians of the trade. The infamous 'Big Bill' Thompson was the mayor of the city, and the south side was the stomping ground of Al Capone. Prohibition was on, and the music was an integral part of the fast-moving, smoky atmosphere of the Speakeasy bar room. State Street was the music scene, and during the twenties, all the big names in blues and jazz could be heard there. King Oliver was known for playing a fine jazz trumpet in the early twenties when he sent for Louis Armstrong in New Orleans to join his band. At the Lincoln Gardens in Chicago, Armstrong's trumpet playing was of such dazzling originality that his influence was to dominate jazz for the next twenty years. His fame became even more widespread when he was joined in 1927 by Earl Hines, an outstanding pianist from Pittsburgh, Pennsylvania.

"The Okeh Record Company was the first to produce Race records in the twenties which helped make the songs of the blues artists accessible in the homes of the people that did not go out to where the music happened. Traveling Victrola salesmen were commonplace, as were records which were sold in corner markets, furniture and hardware stores. Each record had its own 'call number' which would appear in flashy ads appearing in magazines and posters where the records were sold. Okeh published *The Blue Book of the Blues* to publicize its line of black blues artists. Almost all of the blues artists that got to record did so between 1925 and 1930 with companies including Paramount, Okeh and Columbia. This makes it hard to understand things in a continuous spectrum because some guys got to record early in their careers, while others did not record until many years after their greatest influence. Charlie Patton was over forty years old when he made his first record in 1929 called *Pony Blues.* Records could establish an artist at the grass roots level better than playing live to an already devoted crowd. Patton recorded more than other blues artists of his era, with an incredible 42 titles released in a single year! With *That Black Snake Moan* as his trademark recording, Blind Lemon Jefferson recorded 85 sides before his mysterious death in a 1930 Chicago snow storm.

"Brass instruments were often used by popular white composers—Irving Berlin, George Gershwin and Jerome Kern. Brass jazz bands grew larger as the twenties closed and when the thirties rolled around, the popularity of the radio helped to bring the exhilarating pulse of 'swing' to the nation. The statement of a theme, and subsequent variations remained the basic outline for jazz performance, but what grew out of previous development was a tighter, faster-moving, more confident type of ensemble statement. 'Heads' were loose arrangements that the boys knew by heart. There was no

real need to write them down. Jazz was always a vocalized type of music even if it was a lead horn that took up the inflection and pitch contours of the old holler.

"In 1932, Duke Ellington wrote *It Don't Mean A Thing If It Ain't Got That Swing* and the power of his big band proved he meant it. Two years later, Benny Goodman put his band together and, almost overnight, he was crowned 'King of Swing.' Boogie woogie piano was big in the thirties and its greatest exponents were Bill Yancy and Pine Top Smith. This go-for-broke piano style was in the same vein as the barrelhouse piano coming out of Dallas. It was characterized by its non-stop repeating 'walking bass' motif. Smith died in 1929, but influenced the boogie woogie movement years later with his recordings.

"Count Basie brought new heights to the art in the mid-thirties, booking his large jazz group as 'The Band That Played The Blues.' Including guitar technique pioneer Eddie Durham in its ranks, the Basie band refined the large ensemble sound with a lighter, less orchestrated touch. His knockout sax player, Lester Young, made it happen with a new sense of rhythm which broke down distinctions between light and heavy beats. Ella Fitzgerald and Billie Holiday were the most popular female vocalists to emerge onto the jazz scene. Fitzgerald's use of jive 'nonsense syllables' were outlandish and became very popular.

"During the forties, the complex rhythms of Be Bop emerged as a new movement away from the swing era. Dizzie Gillespie's trumpet blew flurries of 16th notes, Charlie Parker's sax was onto some previously unheard of phrasing, and guitarist Charlie Christian was adding altered passing chords never heard in swing. Christian played with Benny Goodman from 1939 to 1941 when, for the first time, he used the electric guitar to play lines that were similar to those used during a horn break. This brought the guitar out of the background from its role of 'boom chang' type strumming, into the same orchestral rank as the trumpet or sax. Jazz guitar players who made their marks were Al Casey, Tiny Grimes, Barney Kessel and the Belgian gypsy, Django Reinhardt.

"If you want to break down the music and look at it cold, much of blues and jazz is the same, with no distinct line between them. When Bessie Smith went to record her blues, the finest jazz guys were always there. Remember that line that we talked about which made the blues, like a simple two-note slide on the low string of Son House's guitar? Well, these jazz guys would dress it up, write it down and blast it out of six horns — all at the same time. That's the difference as I see it.

"Well, it's that straightforward blues guitar that does it for me, Boy. Now, let's get back to the delta and follow the line out; early influences, the blues elements, Charlie Patton, Son House, Robert Johnson. From these pieces come one emerging picture. I'm not saying that it is a straight line. It's far more diverse than that. Just listen to a few more stories and you can draw your own conclusions. One thing is for sure — there were a lot of guys who have gone before us that saw something in that guitar — something that they naturally put their energy behind. I can't tell you what that something is. I only know that it is real.

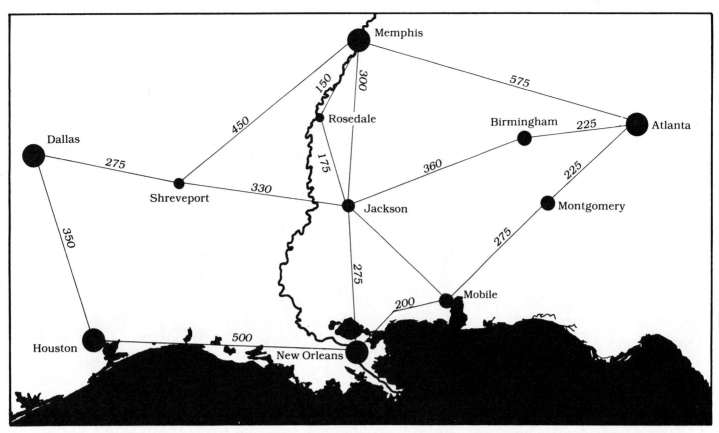

"Son House was known as the best performer in the jukes around Clarksdale in his time. But he is also remembered for his influence on another young delta blues man — Robert Johnson. Johnson's parents didn't want the boy to be exposed to the atmosphere of the neighborhood juke, but he would slip out, and sit at the feet of Son House as he played the evening away. During a break, the boy showed House that he could play harmonica. But when he tried to play guitar, there was no way he could do it. After this frustrating episode, Johnson was not seen for six months. He did return, and with new-found confidence, he sat in with House. According to all that saw it happen, he played some flat-out amazing blues guitar. House was said to reply, 'Well, ain't that fast? He's gone now.'

"Son House was his early influence, but by the time Johnson had traveled all over the east, midwest, south and southwest, he had assimilated many types of guitar styles. He lived fast and hard, and was driven to play. Early on he played a Sears and Roebuck 'stella' guitar, and he had a bad eye that people say made him go all out to prove himself. He took the delta out of the delta. His slashing bottleneck slide was his trademark along with his nervous commanding style. His only recordings are from two Texas sessions in 1938 and 1939. He was more of a musician's musician than he was a popular figure. He traveled with Johnny Shines, another bluesman, and they would roll into town unannounced and play until the people were amazed. Then they'd leave for the next place. His intensity planted the seeds of influence into those who saw him play. Nobody knows exactly how or why he died in 1939, only that it was some trouble that quickly came down. Johnson's life story quickly turned to legend: tormented, genius musician, fast life, confident, vulnerable, early death. Elmore James, the next guy to carry on the tradition, was fortunate enough to tour with Johnson and get his guitar training first hand.

"Prohibition ending in 1933 opened the Chicago clubs once more to advertise the blues performers. Big Bill Broonzy and Sonny Boy Williamson were huge blues figures in the clubs, and Lonnie Johnson and Tampa Red were big recording stars by the end of the thirties.

"Between 1932 and 1934, John and Alan Lomax made an incredible set of recordings for the Archive of American Folk Song for the Library of Congress. With an old Ford, a 350-pound recording machine and two 75-pound batteries, they set out through Texas, Louisiana, Mississippi, Tennessee, Kentucky, Alabama, the Carolinas and Florida. Their goal was to record pure Negro music and they traveled to where the old music was still in the mind of a forgotten people — the prisons, the southern lumber camps and backwoods towns. They ended up with the greatest documentary of Negro folk music ever assembled — recording Leadbelly, Son House and scores of others.

"The forties experienced a communications boom which forever changed the way that music was heard by the public. Chicago, Kansas City, Detroit, St. Louis, Atlanta, Jackson — you name it, the cities had blues music like never before! Juke boxes revolutionized the way that people saw music. They popped up at every crossroad along every highway. They took the place of the performer, and those blues performers that could translate their message onto record took their up-front, rough-edged country into every nook and cranny where people met. Because of World War II, large established record labels like RCA Victor, Bluebird and Decca were hedging their bets with the proven performers. But with the opening of the Jukebox label in 1943, dozens of small labels flourished in the late forties and early fifties. The growth of Negro radio had also come to pass, and audiences grew to unheard-of dimensions all throughout the south.

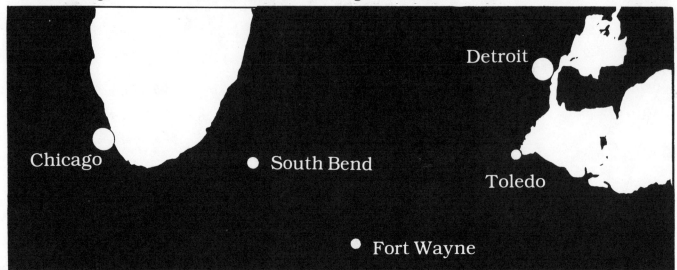

"In Chicago, the word was out on tube amps and the volume levels in the downtown clubs was greater than ever before. Cutting slide guitar came into popularity along with backbeat drumming, crossed harp and screaming vocals. Muddy Waters, Howling Wolf, Little Walter and Willie Dixon were playing their blues in the clubs and among themselves. Robert Nighthawk was out on Maxwell Street singing about going down to 'Eli's Pawn Shop' to deal with some trouble. Elmore James was taking the legend of Robert Johnson into the future. Sizzling slide on the high E, screaming over the back and forth one-two, sure as the sun comes up, he was on that first bar after the twelfth. You could hear it coming just like that train this morning. Rock and Roll was born of this rhythm and blues. T-Bone Walker packed it up in Texas and went out to the west coast to make recordings with his electric guitar. T-Bone used to record with Ida Cox before he set his mind to show his boogie woogie roots. This cat was sophisticated, and his fast-moving use of the blues scale was perfect for the electric.

"These guys had roots alright. But sort of like a Corvette has roots with a Model A Ford. Robert Johnson's influence could clearly be felt in Elmore James' cover of *Dust My Broom* and the famous *Crossroads.* The use of Johnson's works were more than a tribute — they were a basis for James' own career in Chicago. Johnny Shines, who toured with Johnson, was already in Chicago when Muddy Waters arrived there in 1943. John Lee Hooker took the Mississippi tradition to Detroit at the same time. In the decades up to this point, you could see the thread of blues influence grow from one place to another, one person to another, even though it was complicated by the fact that there were several involved. Communication technology and a growing number of artists now made the picture a lot more homogeneous as the rhythm and blues post-war snowball continued to grow in size. They called it jump, boogie, rhythm and blues — whatever you want to call it, one thing is for sure. Nobody was looking back. It was a time of great discovery and freshness.

"WDIA Memphis was the first black-owned and operated radio station in the south when it hired Riley King as a disc jockey. His radio show played between 1948 and 1952 and earned him the name 'Blues Boy' — shortened to just B. B. King. Born in 1925 in Itta Bena, a small delta town near Indianola, Mississippi, his parents lived in a sharecroppers cabin. His single-note lead guitar style was derived from the likes of T-Bone Walker, Charlie Christian and Lonnie Johnson. When his first hit came in 1951 with *Three O'clock Blue,* B. B. was just starting to prove himself as 'The King of the Blues.' Man, when this guy sings, you just know that he means it! His guitar, a cherry red Gibson ES 335 is lovingly referred to as 'Lucille.' When he performs, he says, 'First I sing, then Lucille sings!'

"In 1946 Muddy Waters was first recorded by Aristocrat Records, a white-owned, black oriented company operated by the Chess Brothers in Chicago. At the end of the forties, the company name was changed to Chess and they struck pay-dirt with Muddy's first big hit *Rolling Stone.* Chess came to dominate the Chicago recording scene with Howling Wolf, Little Walter, Sonny Boy Williamson and others signed to their ranks. The direction of the Chess brothers blues-based company took an unexpected turn in 1955 when Muddy Waters pulled Chuck Berry onto the label.

"Something was about to happen that was bigger than anybody knew. The chemistry for a crossover record was ripe and Berry had the driving enthusiastic sound that was one of the key ingredients. White teenagers were showing enthusiasm for the rhythms of blues music; an eclipse was at hand. The radio was ready to publicize a national hit. The juke boxes were geared to the single three-minute recording. And the record distributors were ready to fill the racks with single forty-fives. Chess signed Berry and immediately released *Maybelline.* Leonard Chess made the trip to New York to present the record to Allen Freed, the WABC disc jockey who coined the phrase 'Rock and Roll.' The sales of *Maybelline* were unprecedented, winning the Billboard Triple Award for total sales, radio play and jukebox sales. Blues was the mother, rhythm and blues was the father, availability and white demand was the midwife: Rock and Roll was born.

1950	*Long Gone Lonesome Blues*	Hank Williams
1951	*How High The Moon*	Les Paul and Mary Ford
1952	*Lawdy Miss Clawdy*	Lloyd Price
1953	*The Clock*	Johnny Ace
1954	*The Things That I Used To Do*	Guitar Slim
1955	*Maybelline*	Chuck Berry
1956	*Heartbreak Hotel*	Elvis Presley
1957	*Peggy Sue*	Buddy Holly
1958	*Johnny B. Goode*	Chuck Berry
1959	*What'd I Say*	Ray Charles
1960	*Walk Don't Run*	The Ventures
1961	*Please Mr. Postman*	Marvelettes
1962	*He's A Rebel*	Crystals
1963	*Hitchhike*	Marvin Gaye
1964	*I Want To Hold Your Hand*	The Beatles
1965	*Like a Rolling Stone*	Bob Dylan
1966	*Paint It Black*	The Rolling Stones
1967	*Are You Experienced*	The Jimi Hendrix Experience

"At about this time the same hand was being dealt in Memphis. It was in this city that Sam Phillips, a white former radio engineer, started the Sun record label in 1952 after several years of helping unknown struggling black artists like Bobby Bland, Little Junior Parker and Walter Horton get a start. In 1954, Phillips recorded 19-year-old Elvis Presley doing a cover of Arthur 'Big Boy' Crudup's *That's All Right,* a traditional blues song. Born on January 8, 1935 in Tupelo, Mississippi, the lone survivor of twins, Elvis claimed that 'since I was two years old all I knew was gospel music. That was music to me.' By the time that his second record came out, *Good Rocking Tonight* he was on tour through Mississippi and Texas performing a rough-and-ready singing act at school houses and dance halls. After his first year out, Elvis was named 8th most promising new hillbilly artist in a 1954 Billboard poll.

"Early on, Elvis was carrying on the blues tradition in lifestyle if not in song. You would not have recognized him when he took the stage those hot summer nights in Texas after the country and western swing band had finished their last number. Like jumping off a moving train, he would scope out the ground below, then make the move. He was beside himself in discovering his own transcendence. He was in top form, out to prove, and in his own personal way, was reckless. This is what made him attractive to the huge white audience who were doing the straight and narrow of their parents' world. This guy was coming in from the side and was making it! The story goes that he fell into his first great fast moving rock numbers between takes of trying to get behind some stuffy gospel ballad. Sounds like what happened to Handy in that Clarksdale theatre when he got the call to 'play it loose.' The same technology that made Elvis visible to the mass market made him, more than anything else, a symbol of a dream to break free. In January of 1956, he signed with RCA in Nashville and went on to make fourteen consecutive million-sellers. In 1958 Elvis went into the army and it was all over. His music would never be the same.

"The American blues scene was put on hold by the developments of the mid-fifties and innovative directions were being sought away from the confines of the past. In 1959, Miles Davis put together his recording session for 'Kind of Blue,' which set new guidelines for improvising. John Coltrain was included and the use of a preset series of modal scales influenced his subsequent work.

"The same year that Elvis gave up music for Uncle Sam, Muddy Waters stepped off the airplane in London, England, and with him went a century of American music. United States soldiers had left a lot of blues records behind in England after the war, and once the interest for blues was sparked, a lot more records were sold mail order through record companies such as Chess in Chicago.

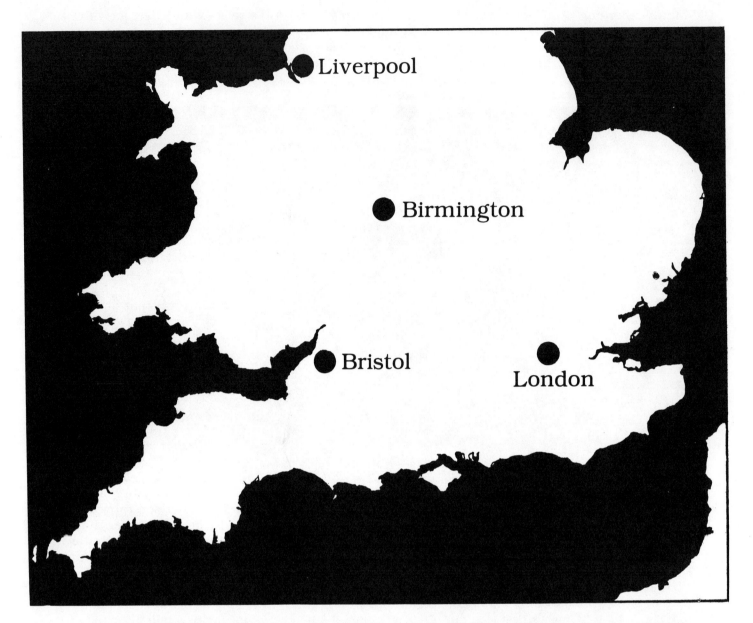

Liverpool

Birmington

Bristol

London

"The youth of England looked to America for a deep folk music tradition that was already developed. Believe it or not, there was a resurgence of the New Orleans jazz band tradition in England in the fifties. More importantly, there were a few young English musicians who embraced the guitar styles of the American bluesmen of the thirties. Alexis Korner and Cyril Davis were two such Englishmen who got together in 1960 with a young slide player named Brian Jones, and later formed a unique group called Blues Incorporated. Brian Jones soon gravitated to two other blues players — Keith Richard and Mick Jagger — and the Rolling Stones were formed. They did strictly blues in the beginning, taking their name from Muddy's first hit with Chess. Brian couldn't get enough of the Elmore James sound, Keith loved Chuck Berry, and Mick had an extensive blues record collection. Yeah, even though these guys grew up closer to Paris than to Memphis, I guess we'll let 'em pass. They did great covers of Muddy's *I Just Want To Make Love To You* and Robert Johnson's *Love in Vain.* After their 1966 album *Aftermath,* they evolved into their own thing, but they'll always remain in debt to the blues form.

"The Yardbirds were another English group with deep blues roots. They are legendary today for having spawned three electric guitarists that went on to write rock history: Jeff Beck, Jimmy Page and Eric Clapton. Clapton next played with John Mayall and the Bluesbreakers, who played strict blues standards. When this band played a number that spotlighted Eric on guitar, you could hear some of the most disciplined, authentic and flashy lead guitarwork on either side of the Atlantic. Clapton then went on to lead the three-man group Cream who did versions of early blues standards like *Roll and Tumble, Outside Woman Blues* and *Sitting on Top of the World.* Another great guitarist from John Mayall's group is Mick Taylor who eventually became lead guitarist in the Stones. Listen to *Get Your Ya Ya's Out* for an earful of blues technique.

"Back in America, the folk purists were 'rediscovering' their own roots by resurrecting from obscurity a few of the surviving bluesmen from the thirties such as Mississippi John Hurt, Skip James, Son House and Bukka White. The blues tradition was being carried on by a few white Chicago boys by the name of Mike Bloomsfield, a guitarist who devoted himself to the blues, and Paul Butterfield, who played an incredible harp on the south side.

"I really should mention Duane Allman, the Georgian slide guitarist who earned himself a reputation in both blues and rock by playing on Clapton's *Layla* album. Roy Buchannan and guitarist Johnny Winter can still blaze with the best of them, as can slide guitarist George Thorogood from Newark, Delaware.

"Although he wasn't known for it, Jimi Hendrix could play blues guitar so as to make Charlie, Son, Robert, Elmore and T-Bone all cry and testify. If you don't believe me, give a listen to *Red House* on his best hits album. Jimi, like Charlie Patton, was not completely Negro. He was one-quarter Cherokee Indian. Jimi played the 'Chittlen Circuit' through the south with innumerable black soul and rhythm and blues type bands. He probably saw as many dirt towns and southern railway stations as Blind Lemon. Hanging out in a Chicago recording studio in the mid-sixties, he crossed paths with Muddy Waters. He played the dives around the Apollo in Harlem just like the classic blues singers of the twenties. He would wake up in Greenwich Village with nothing but a guitar leaning against a single bed and a promise to play the blues in a small club down the street that night. No need to hang your head Jimi, not like your forefathers in that dirt road shack. Somebody's going to walk right through that door and give you a brand new white Fender guitar. You only think that you are alone, but there were others before in the same deal. Now your blind faith is going to pay off, and you will be free in your art.

"During the summer of 1967, Jimi played the 'Monterey Pop Festival' in California. It was his chance to prove himself — his chance to live — his chance to play the blues. After an hour of guitar-work that left the suntanned crowd stunned and crying for more, Jimi set his guitar on fire as a symbol for all to see. His one love was in flames, his blues were real."

That was it. The old man would say no more. He quietly stepped off the tracks and slowly walked toward a path that went into the surrounding woods. The boy stood still between the rails and just looked down at his feet as the sky turned purple with the setting sun. After a few moments, the boy walked to catch up to the old man on the dirt trail, and upon reaching him, they walked together quietly for several minutes. Feeling a need to break the silence, the boy spoke out directly. "Well how about it Old Man?" The old man slowly looked over at the boy with his eyes smiling. "Are you going to teach me how to crackerjack?"

They both laughed as the old man pointed his finger to a campsite down the path.

2. The Beat

Flames danced into the air within the ring of rocks that outlined the firesite. The night was quiet and the boy sat eagerly across from the old man who held his guitar across one leg. "Now get yourself settled and tune into what I'm going to say, because I'm going to tell you about the beat time that is necessary for building up a blues song. Don't get too anxious to learn the best riffs right off. Remember, quiet time comes first. After a while you'll see that we have come full circle, and then you will have the overall picture. We have to build, so let's just recognize that we are at the beginning and that we must take up a fair number of related subjects one at a time until we start to see the whole picture, I don't know any other way to do it.

ESTABLISHING THE BEAT

"O. K., what's in the beat? Well, you can't see it, so you have to understand it by knowing its sound. The first thing you do is snap your fingers nice and even."

D-1 Snap   Snap   Snap   Snap

The old man's fingers sparked out a smooth regular interval. "Don't even count 'em. Just think of each snap as its own. Put a moderate, even space between each one and what do you have? The basic beat. This simple skeleton is underneath all of the music that makes up a song. You can take away the lead guitar and the singer's voice, the piano and the bass line. Even if you take the drummer's work and break it down, here is what you'll get after the last veil has been lifted. For now, picture a common, easy beat, just what the hand can easily do. Now, what is the next thing to look at?

GROUPING THE BEAT

"It is grouping the beats. So how are we to do that? Well in a sense we have already done it because by not counting with numbers at all we put a one count on every beat. Let's start now with counting two beats to a group. This is known as a double beat, but I call it the old 'tick-tock.' It goes like this:

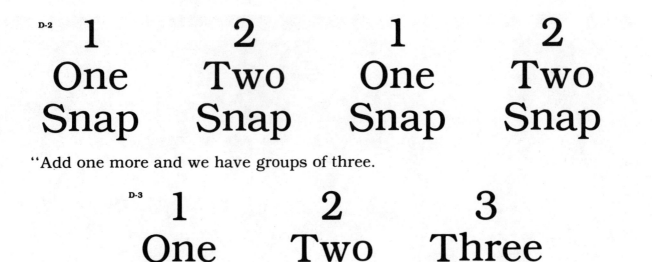

D-2

1	**2**	**1**	**2**
One	Two	One	Two
Snap	Snap	Snap	Snap

"Add one more and we have groups of three.

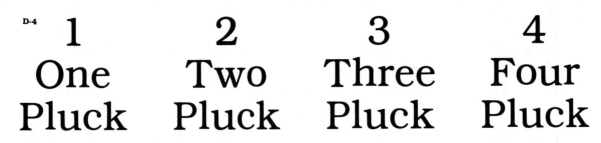

D-3

1	**2**	**3**
One	Two	Three
Snap	Snap	Snap

"You with me, Boy?" The boy sharpened his attention, but could not hide his impatience. "Maybe if I do the four count on the bottom string, that would wake you up." Counting out loud and plucking the lowest string the old man sent the beat out of the guitar.

D-4

1	**2**	**3**	**4**
One	Two	Three	Four
Pluck	Pluck	Pluck	Pluck

"There is always an equal amount of time between all of the beats, no matter what their number, so right after four, you go back to one. You see, the beat is a point in time and has no real duration of its own. The four count is far and away the count that you will use the most. But you can have more than four beats to a measure in certain cases. So what are you going to do with your four count, Boy? Your wheel with four evenly placed spokes that roll around.

BAR LINES

"The words 'bar' or 'measure' are used when we consider the beats contained in any one group. In the four count measure, we are considering the elapsed time between beat one and the first beat of the next measure. Measures are designated on the common musical staff by 'bar lines' which are vertical lines that run through all lines on the staff from top to bottom. They allow you to count bars or measures as we once counted individual beats. Here is what the bar lines look like:

D-5

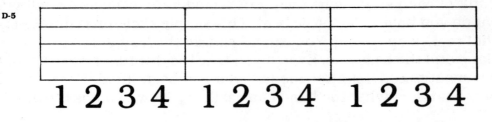

1 2 3 4   1 2 3 4   1 2 3 4

"So, first you count the beats, then you group them into bars. In a short while, we will see how you can count the bars into groups, usually of twelve, so you can come back to an original starting point after a certain number of bars roll by.

ACCENT

"The next thing is the accenting of particular beats in the measure. There are three ways in which you can accent any single beat. You can stress a beat by making it louder than the surrounding beats; or if you are considering a note played on the beat, you can make it higher in pitch or longer in duration than the other beat notes. [See appendix 1]. The most common way to accent the four count is by making the first beat a bit louder than the rest. Another way that you'll hear it is with a secondary accent on the third beat.

$$\overset{\displaystyle V}{1} \quad 2 \quad \overset{\displaystyle v}{3} \quad 4$$

D-6

"Of course, drummers are not called upon to be perfect clocks. We are only looking at a blueprint example to account for all the things we know can happen. Blues recordings show us that in order to get feeling out of the rhythm, drummers commonly employ a technique called 'syncopation,' which highlights the weaker beats, usually the second and the fourth in the four count, or skip over the strong beats to throw some tension into the scheme. Some embellishments cannot be studied by sitting down and talking about them because they happen too fast and are asymetric to the strict pattern, lagging slightly off the calculated beat mark. I'm just filling you in so you will know what the drummer might do when it is your turn to play guitar.

TEMPO

"The next thing is the tempo. This is essentially the rate of speed of the beat or the duration of time between each of the common beats. My first example of the regularly-timed finger snap could be considered a moderate beat. But that regular beat is only part of a spectrum that swings from slow to fast. [Appendix 2] If we shorten the time between beats, everything gets proportionally faster and the bars will go by at an increased rate. The opposite is true for the slow drag beats.

D-7

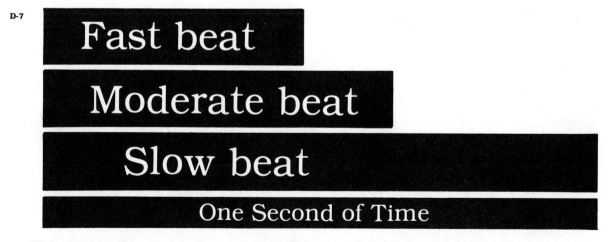

"It's not really as simple as it seems because changing the tempo has some consequences that are not immediately evident. If you take one song and play it at different tempos, you will notice that there's a lot more time to work out your playing when the beat is slow. The faster tempo is more demanding, especially for chord workings. It is important to be aware of tempo if you seem stuck with a song that doesn't seem to work. Change it around a little bit, speed it up, or slow it down. You will find that it changes the complexion of the piece. Sometimes the tempo of a song is purposefully accelerated or slowed down for effect. But don't let this happen when you don't want it to. The first thing a blues man has to have is a deep sense of steady rhythm. Develop the ability to keep the tempo going even if it is not sounded. Built-in beat — that's what you need to pull off the best moves. If you ever feel lost for inspiration when you are playing, just take it down to that basic count. Never think that simple isn't what you want. I'll show you how to play your line right over that beat. But for now, let's get into the beat a little deeper.

DIVISION OF THE BEAT

"The next thing at hand is the division of the beat. I started with snapping my fingers and then grouped the snaps into a larger category. Now we are going to break down the time interval between snaps. Keeping with our four count as an example, let's divide each beat into two parts.

D-8
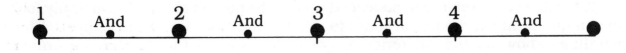

"When the beats are counted out loud, this minor division is usually designated by the word 'and' placed between each numbered count. Sub-division does not usually affect the prominance of the major beats. So a four count divided into smaller parts is still a four count — even though you will sometimes hear the phrase 'Eight to the bar' to mean four count with one subdivision between each beat. The next breakdown is to take the beat down into three parts counting 'and da' between each numbered count.

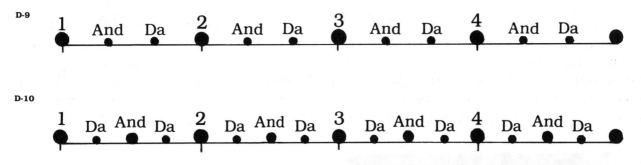

"This triple subdivision is often used with slower blues tempos to fill out the beat and to give an odd number feel to an otherwise evenly numbered structure. The words 'da and da' are used to divide the beat into quarters.

"These multiple divisions are often used to spread out the beat on the slower tempos and can fool you by hiding the original beat. After a few seconds of listening and snapping your fingers, you can usually identify the four count as the underlying structure."

The old man stood up to put another log on the fire and asked the boy to pick up his guitar. "Talking through the air is all well and good, Boy, but have you understood what I have said?"

"I think I see the picture," said the boy.

"Then play for me, using only the bottom string of the guitar, a fast tempo playing every beat." Out of the box came the beat. "Now accent the first and third beat on a moderate tempo." Once again the string obeyed. "Now give me a triple divided beat using a slow tempo with an accent on the first beat only." Even though it was just one string being sounded, the campsite was filled with the prescribed rhythm.

Staring down into the flames, the old man said, "Just checking, Boy."

3. The Note

acing a circle around the fire, the old man demanded the boy's full attention. "The basic difference between a beat and a note is their duration in time. The beat is but a point — a single wave of disturbance traveling once through the air. The note is created by a vibrating mass — a string in the case of the guitar — which sets a series of sound waves into motion which continue to be emitted until the source of the disturbance stops vibrating. If the beat were a single locomotive roaring down the tracks, then the note would be the whole freight train. The two basic characteristics of a note are pitch and duration. The pitch of a note is determined by the rate of the vibrating mass, which, depending on if it is fast or slow, makes the note sound high or low. Compared to pitch, duration is a more humanly-determined characteristic because it depends on how long we decide to let the instrument create the note. I will tell you all you need to know about pitch and the nature of sound in a short while. Let's concentrate on the duration of a note for now.

THE QUARTER NOTE

"The idea of using a note to make music immediately ties it to the rhythm of the song, which in turn brings us back to the beat structure. The direct relationship between the beat and the length of time which the note is played is the next thing that I want you to understand. The four count is made up of four evenly spaced beats. Let's start with playing a constant, unvarying note between the first two beats.

D-11

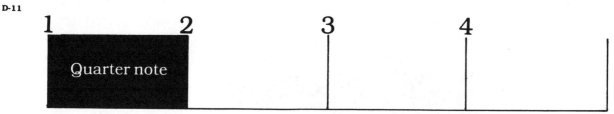

Quarter note

"Now we have established a certain time period for our note. Now hear this: a note which sounds for the time between two common beats is called a quarter note. This is the most commonly found time value for a note in a melody or instrumental passage. I guess that they could have just as easily called it a whole note, or a purple note. But they didn't. So, the first thing that you are being introduced to is the quarter note — which lasts the time between any two beats. Tempo throws a curve ball into the game by making the distance between beats fall within a range of long to short. This means that quarter notes from two songs with different tempos are not the same in terms of measured time. They vary according to the distance between beats. The idea of a quarter note is a concept — it's not really a determined length of time on a stopwatch.

"Once you understand what a quarter note is, you might like to know that there is an entire system of written music which follows directly from this concept of a timed note. The system for reading music on the common five line staff can be a very involved process. But I will only show you what I think is necessary in order for you to play your guitar with confidence. I want you to understand a few things about the common system as a primer to learning the special six line guitar staff which I will use to show you guitar passages.

OTHER NOTE VALUES

"In order to make notes that are longer or shorter in time than a quarter note, you either multiply or divide the quarter note's time value by two. Remember the 'and' that I used to subdivide the beat into two? Well, a note played from the first beat to this half-way division will take on the value of an eighth note. This is a note one half of a beat in duration. Likewise, a half note is the value of time across two full beats, and a whole note is the time that it takes to count through an entire four count measure.

D-12

"Each different time-valued note has its own symbol placed either on or between the lines of the common five line staff. This symbol indicates the note's pitch and duration. Pitch is shown by the note's vertical position on the staff. Duration is shown by the note symbol used.

TIME SIGNATURE

"A time signature is a figure used in the beginning of a song to give a musician information about the meter or timing structure. This is done with a symbol that looks like a fraction. The upper figure gives you the number of beats in a bar or measure. The lower figure tells you the type of note in which these beats are expressed. The four count that we have used so far can now be called 4/4 time because it has four separate quarter notes to the bar or measure. There are lots of possibilities for time signature [Appendix 3] like 2/4, 3/4, 6/8, but for blues and most popular music, 4/4 time is the most commonly used meter. Because of its

D-13

prominence, 4/4 is called 'common time' and is designated by a C or 4/4 at the beginning of the piece.

"If you have a song that is in 4/4 time, then in between any two bar lines that define a measure, you will find what amounts to the time of four quarter notes or one whole note. A 4/4 measure could be taken up with four quarter notes, one half and two quarters, one whole note — whatever fills the space.

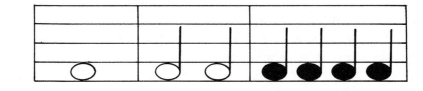

D-14

"There are also a series of rest symbols that are used in order to fill in the empty time left if there is a pause in a measure. For each time valued note symbol, there is also an equivalent rest symbol. Both time values and rests are used on the five line staff to fill in the total time value of a measure.

"Here is the problem as I see it. The student comes along and wants to learn how to play a hot guitar. But the first thing that a teacher gives him to work with is a lot of foreign symbols and lines and rest stops and none of it makes any real sense. A lot of guys stop right at this point because there seems to be a wall that you have to climb before you can even start to get it rolling. Well, the music was there first, then somebody came along and put it into all of these different catagories with varying symbols and concepts. We have these extremes of playing by ear and the stuffy formality of what we will call the common sight-reading system.

"The common system evolved over several centuries and has a very intricate method for putting down every little thing about a piece of music. It was designed around a major scale of seven notes, and is very useful for large orchestra arrangements which have written music for twenty or thirty parts. This system works well for classical music and popular forms, but does not lend itself completely to the loose improvising picture that is needed for blues guitar. First of all, the blues works out of a five note scale which throws a wrench right in the middle of the works set up for a seven note major scale. Secondly, the common system is not oriented to the beat visually. It does not use a horizontal direction of the staff as an equally measured time line. A whole note and an eighth note take up the same space on the line, but one is to be held eight times longer than the other. Thirdly, the whole thing is unnecessarily complex for the blues guitarist. Did you know that the correct name for a sixty-fourth note rest stop is a 'hemisemidemiquaver?' When Elmore James broke into *Dust My Broom,* was he thinking of this stuff? Oh, don't get me wrong, *The Dictionary of Music* is one of my favorite books because it is all out there between two covers, and I really admire the guys that figured the system out and can use it. If you are going to play ragtime piano, you better start reading music from square one. I just think that learning the basics and listening closely to an hour of blues records is more like it. Know what I mean, jellybean?

SPECIAL SIX LINE GUITAR STAFF

"Anyway, what I'm getting at is the special guitar staff that I want you to use. I worked it out after a long trial period, and I believe that it manages to bring together the best of both worlds. Just like blues guitar music, it does not present an absolute picture, but a working approximation of what is to be played. Here is the lowdown.

"The word 'transcription' will be used to describe an example given on the six line staff. The example given here shows the sequence of notes that result when an E major chord is strummed from the low E string to the high E string. Symbols that are used to indicate a particular technique and various dot sizes with relative values are also shown."

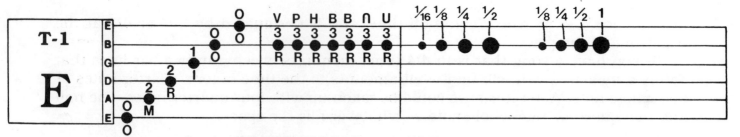

● The lines of the staff represent the six strings of the guitar the way they would appear if the guitar were on your lap with the body of the guitar on your right leg. The note played by each open string is identified at the opening of the transcription. The bottom of the six lines represents the low E string and each ascending line represents the next higher string.

● The appearance of a dot on a line means that a note is to be sounded on the corresponding string. There are four dot sizes referred to as small, medium, large and extra large — each of which represent one of a consecutive progression of time value steps comparable to the quarter note system. Dot size will be gauged to time value according to how a dot is first shown to work with the beat. The dot size appearing directly on the beat will represent quarter notes. The important thing is to see the relative steps from one size to another. For a passage where all the notes have the same value, the medium size is used throughout.

● A four count beat is measured under the six lines of most staffs by an evenly segmented, numbered line. This will tune you into the beat and where the notes will take place in the four count measure.

● A letter appearing below each dot indicates the finger of the left hand to be used in fretting the note. These letters are 'I' for index, 'M' for middle, 'R' for ring, and 'P' for pinky. An 'O' appears on strings to be played open and an 'X' appears on strings not played or muted.

● Seven symbols are used to indicate specific techniques and appear above or between the notes involved. Explanations of the various techniques are given as they are introduced.

Symbol	Technique
P	Pull
H	Hammer
V	Vibrato
B	Bend half step
● B	Bend whole step
U	Slide up
∩	Slide down

"A dot next to the bend symbol indicates that the string used is to be bent to sound the note normally played two frets above the original. Without the dot, bend only enough to raise tone one half step or one fret. All transcriptions are numbered and labeled for key. Not all transcriptions have the beat count line under the six regular lines, but those that don't are linear passages and can be understood without the measured count. In this case, assign any value to the middle size dot, and when you see the large size, just double the duration of the time value given to the middle size dot. This is the principle behind the different size dots. The small guy is half as long as the middle size, and the middle size is half as long as the large dot. On a transcription where all the notes have the same time value, the medium size dot is used.

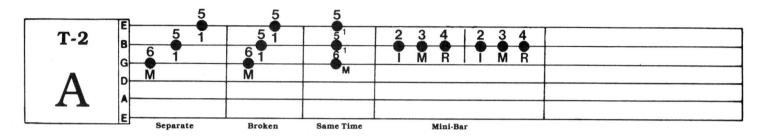

"Take a look at this transcription and you will see the three ways that I take care of notes that are played together. The first group shows three notes that are played successively — each independent of each other. The second indicates that the notes are played immediately after one another in a 'broken' chord fashion. The third way shows the notes stacked and indicates that the notes are to be played 'simultaneously' in a single, quick movement of the pick. The final grouping shows a set of two triplets with a mini-bar between them.

"On the transcriptions that do use the numbered beat bar, the six line transcription will take on the properties of a time line which moves from left to right — so look for the small dots to be grouped together, with spaces following the larger dots. Description can go on forever. The important thing is just to use the transcriptions that I give you until you can 'read' them from beginning to end. With the exception of the complete twelve bar example, I will give you shorter passages of ten or fifteen notes which you will find easy to picture as separate pieces. Listen, I don't want to hear that you can't use the transcriptions until you really try your best to work with them. The beginning is the hardest part — so spend some time with them and you will get the hang."

The rays from the early morning sun were beginning to break through onto the white ashes that were the night's campfire. "We've been up all night!" the boy exclaimed.

"Yes, Boy, if you are interested enough in what you're doing, your body will provide energy that you never knew it had. Come and pick yourself up. Let's move on to another place I know of where I can teach you more about the notes we use to make the blues."

They walked together along a path adjacent to the tracks until an old wood frame house appeared in a nearby field.

The new day brought a renewed feeling of wonderment to the boy. Just twenty-four hours before he was walking out of the city alone with his guitar, mysteriously drawn to the presence of the old man. "How can it be that things can change so much in one day?"

The old man answered in an unbroken gentle tone. "Well, it's like the lake behind a dam. It might take quite a while to fill up, but when the dam breaks, that water will go where it knows it has to. Now just because it happened, don't think it so strange. Just prepare for more changes as you go. It is only the mind that makes things familiar. Everything outside the mind runs on extremely strict rules which concern chemical repulsion, attraction and light phenomena. If you think about it hard enough, it will all come clear to you some day. It's easier to just play along with the games that some people play. But don't ever believe for a second that anybody really ever owns anything. You might pull up next to something for a while, but it is not yours."

The old man led the way up to the old house which stood on a few acres cleared from the woods. "Is this your house, Old Man?"

"You might say that. We are free to stay here as long as we progress in our music study." The old man had a way of getting to the point that constantly amazed the boy. It seemed the old man was always in a ready frame of mind, slowing only to make sure of the boy's attention. "Fill yourself with energy, Boy, and pay close attention. I will tell you more about the music."

They sat on the old wood porch which surrounded the back of the house and overlooked the land that slowly descended down to the tracks.

"One of the big problems that keeps us from understanding our situation is the fact that we are limited by our size and senses. The unseen, be it too large or too small, is still there whether you like it or not, Boy. You're stuck in the middle of the range."

The boy sat transfixed, waiting for the next words to come through the air.

4. The Range We Live

Galaxies are known to number more than 10-billion. The Milky Way Galaxy, the one we call home, has about 200-billion individual stars which turn together like a giant wheel completing one revolution every 250-million years. Our yellow day sun is one of these stars, and is about 93,000,000 miles away from our tiny planet called Earth. Now if you squint real hard through the clouds, Boy, you can see the Mississippi delta laying the water low as it comes down out of the highlands. It just so happens to be that this planet was the right size and had the right conditions to have an atmosphere which is a gaseous mass surrounding a celestial body. It is the gravity of the earth that pulls this gas to the surface, and although we don't perceive it because we evolved in it, there is a considerable pressure at the planet's surface which results from the molecules of gas being drawn to the center of the planet's mass. This pressurized gas is composed of 78 percent nitrogen, 21 percent oxygen, .9 percent argon, and others.

"What I'm getting at is this: if you hold your hand out in front of your eyes, there are billions of air molecules between your hand and your eyes. You can't trust your eyes, so blow on your hand and feel it. Well, one of the secrets to understanding acoustics — the science of sound — is to think of these molecules in the atmosphere as being in constant motion and immediately next to each other in space.

ACOUSTICS — THE SCIENCE OF SOUND

"Now, let's add up a few things. Let's say that we hit the top of a snare drum and you hear it. The stick hits the drumhead making it move, then the surface of the head moves the molecules immediately against it setting up a wave of disturbance which moves away from the drum in all directions. Now remember, just like twenty beach balls on the surface of a swimming pool only move up and down as a wave goes by, so the molecules in the gas transmit the wave as one molecule smashes into the adjacent molecule. Under equal temperature and pressure the rate of movement of the sound wave is the same for all sounds at about 740 miles per hour. The volume of the sound is a function of the degree of disturbance, but loud or soft, all

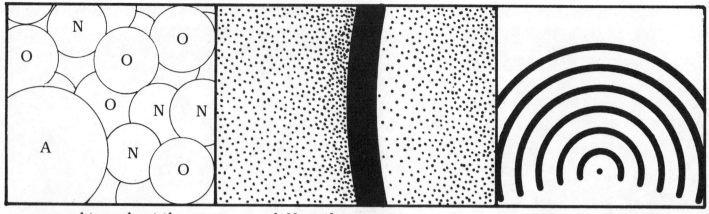

sound travels at the same speed. Now these pressure waves are going away from the drumhead in three dimensions through the gas as your ear scoops in a little. The surface of the ear drum is moved by the change in pressure created by the pressure variations of the wave. As far as hearing is concerned, this is the end of the line for the waves in the gas. From this point in, the impulse is carried through a series of steps which use bone and fluid to carry the vibration to the organ of hearing — the organ of Corti. This dude has about 23,000 small hair follicles, each of which is activated by a very limited range of vibration. These hairs meet up with special nerve endings that go directly to the brain where sound is finally perceived.

"We know that a note is created by a vibrating mass. This could be a guitar string, the reed of a saxophone, a tuning fork — whatever you hear. The neat thing about the vibrating mass that is employed for musical instruments is the fact that they sustain the vibration in one way or another. With the sax you use lung power to exhale a stream of moving air over the reed. The guitar sounds from the plucking of the string, and the sustain is created by the body of the guitar holding the vibrating string taunt. The body of the guitar shakes the molecules of gas as does the surface of the string, which is in violent motion relative to the wood of the guitar.

"The electric guitar amplifier shakes the air in huge physical quantities compared to the way that strings do. You see, the electric guitar is quite another beast altogether. This monster actually feeds on itself. It can get so sensitive that you actually have to hold the strings from feeding back. Because of the magnetic electric story behind how the pick-up and strings work together, only metal strings work on electric guitars. We'll talk about guitarists around post-war Chicago and how they exploited the electric after we travel for awhile. Right now, let's get back to sound waves from the vibrating mass.

"A single drum beat sets essentially one wave into motion. The vibrating mass of a string, by beating the air next to it again and again, sets off a series of waves. Here is the lowdown — the speed at which the mass vibrates is called the frequency, and this determines the pitch of the note. This means high frequency/high note, low frequency/low note. The amplitude is the second measureable characteristic we will note about a vibrating mass. This is the extent of movement in any one given cycle of the vibrating mass. Look down at your low E string and hit it hard, then hit it soft and you will see for yourself the height of the string vibration. Needless to say, this determines the volume. Electric guitarists are known to face their amps to let the sound waves from the speakers increase the amplitude of their already singing strings. Rather than decay, which you always get from a plucked acoustic guitar string, the electric is capable of increasing sustain.

"Now, let's go, Boy. We know that the string is vibrating very fast, and we know that it is producing an audible sound, so we have pitch and loudness from the note. The subject of duration is already in our file.

THE RANGE OF HUMAN HEARING

"The next question at hand is how slowly or rapidly the source may vibrate and still be detected by the ear. When a sound source is vibrating at lower than twenty cycles per second, one hears the separate waves in an oscillating swoosh as they go in the ear. This is the bottom of the range of human hearing. Above this frequency, a continuous tone is perceived and as the rate of vibration increases, the pitch increases accordingly. This is the range I want you to understand, Boy. At one point it is too low to hear. At another it is too high, too fast. Now, at 1,000 cycles per second, we hear approximately the sound of a soprano's high C. This is a high note for a singer, but don't draw any conclusions about the range of human hearing from this fact. The top of a human's hearing range extends over 20,000 cycles per second before you simply can't hear anymore. The ear is not equally sensitive to all frequencies, but works best between 1,000 and 4,000 cycles per second. Now, don't get too excited, Boy. We are going to clear this up if you hold on."

THE OCTAVE

The old man sat up straight and sang out a clear, unvarying note. "Now I happen to know that the note I just sang was 440 cycles per second. This frequency has been established as an A note. Now, with my voice, I will slide the pitch from this established note into higher frequencies."

The boy sat back as the old man's voice sounded a smooth curve of steadily increasing pitch. The boy could hear familiar notes go by like station stops on a train headed for its destination. At one point, the old man looked into the boy's eyes to get his strict attention. As he raised the pitch of his voice, the old man slowly brought his hands closer and closer together. Something was happening with the sound, but the boy couldn't quite figure it out. In a moment of resolve, the old man brought his hands together and the boy spoke out impulsively. "You're singing the same note that you started with!"

The old man caught his breath, but started right in. "How could that be, Boy? How can I sing the same note by singing higher and higher to get to it? The answer lies in the phenomenon known as the octave. The Greek philosopher, Pythagoras, figured this same thing out long ago with his voice. Just like a foot ruler measures one foot and then another on top of that, the octave divides the range of human hearing into identifiable repeating cycles.

"This is no accident that is just happening to you, Boy. The game works out mathematically on paper, too. Now I told you that the first note that I sang was 440 cycles per second. Well, the point where you heard the distinctive higher note — that is the octave of the lower note — was when my voice box created a vibration in the atmosphere of exactly 880 cycles per second, precisely twice that of the starting point.

"You said that my singing had arrived at the 'same note' as the one I started with. Well, in a way, you are right, and in a way you are wrong. The higher note was indeed another A note, checking in at 880 cycles per second. But was it the same note? Not really. There is only one 440 A note. Those two notes are brothers in the family of A notes. This doubling of measured cycles per second marks the repetition of the octave throughout the range of human hearing. Now, if we know that the octave spans the distance between two notes where one is twice the vibration rate of the other, how many octaves are in the range of human hearing if we can hear between 20 and 20,000 cycles per second?

"It boils down to about ten octaves. Each musical instrument takes up a part of this range. The piano's range is a little over seven octaves, encompassing approximately 30 to 4,000 cycles per second. The guitar takes up four octaves in its range and, unlike the piano or saxophone, can play the same note on another string at a different position on the instrument.

"Yes, octaves are starting points that have multiple frequencies by a factor of two and are interspersed through the range that we hear. This doubling of the number takes a while to get used to because the numbers get larger at an accelerated rate. On the low side of the range, there is an entire octave between 20 and 40 cycles per second. On the other end of the spectrum, half of the range of human hearing is encompassed in the last octave that we hear. Just stare at these two charts for a while and you will get the picture.

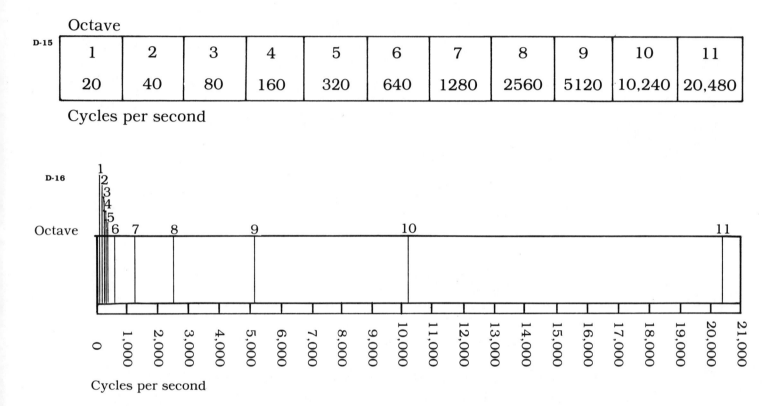

Octave

D-15

1	2	3	4	5	6	7	8	9	10	11
20	40	80	160	320	640	1280	2560	5120	10,240	20,480

Cycles per second

Cycles per second

ESTABLISHMENT OF THE MAJOR SCALE

"Now, let's look at how musicians broke down the distance between any two octaves into a series of scale steps. If we are talking octaves, we have already established a starting point and we know that to be 440 cycles per second."

The old man reached over onto a nearby table and picked up a small box with a dial and a speaker built into it. "This dial is set to sweep between the points 440 and 880 cycles per second. You can turn the dial to any point between these two octave marks, and you can hear the resulting pitch from the speaker. There are certainly lots of different ways to divide the distance between two octaves. But since we are both familiar with the 'Do, Re, Mi' major scale, let's jump right into that. The major scale is a diatonic scale which has seven scale degrees. Counting the octave mark as the first of the scale, the major has six stop-over points that divide the range of the single octave. Now, what I want you to do is to turn the dial on the box up from the first of the scale, the 440 'Do' note, until you hear the second of the scale, the 'Re' note, and stop exactly at that point so we can see the frequency number of the second."

The boy turned the dial slowly until the pitch made by the speaker was the familiar "Re" note. "Now, continue up the scale, stopping exactly on the point of the other scale steps.'' Mi, Fa, Sol, La, Ti and Do were measured. "You seem to have pretty good ears, Boy. I wrote down all of the numbers from the dial as you ascended through the scale and here is what I came up with.

D-17

1 Do 440	2 Re 494	3 Mi 554	4 Fa 587	5 Sol 659	6 La 740	7 Ti 831	8 Do 880

"Now, if we take the frequency reading for any one scale degree and mathematically work it against the number of the opening 440 tonic note, we come up with a ratio number. This is a top heavy fraction that you multiply against the 440 tonic to get the frequency number of a particular scale degree. These ratio figures can be used to figure out the frequency of scale degrees between any two octave marks.

D-18

	1 A'	2	3	4	5	6	7	8 (1) A''
Frequency in terms of tonic f	f	9/8f	5/4f	4/3f	3/2f	5/3f	15/8f	2f
Ratio between successive frequencies		9/8 Major tone	10/9 Minor tone	16/15 Semi tone	9/8 Major tone	10/9 Minor tone	9/8 Major tone	16/15 Semi tone

"When a carpenter puts in a stairwell between floors, he usually designs about fourteen steps each of which are seven inches in height. You just divided up the octave into seven steps, using three different sizes of steps. It works out that two of the steps are almost the same size, the third one is just about half the size of the two larger varieties. The major tone is the largest and there are three of them starting with the step between 'Do' and 'Re.' The minor tone is slightly smaller and there are two of these between the second and third and the fifth and sixth. The semi-tone is about half as large as the other two and fits between the third and fouth, and the seventh and the first of the scale.

"This method of presenting the major scale is called 'just temperament' because it is true both mathematically and to the ear in its establishment of degree relative to the tonic note. Here's the rub. This system works great when you are whistling *Dixie* using only major scale degrees. But when you try to subdivide a major or minor tone into half to get an intermediate passing tone, the trouble begins. You have to establish two distinctly different notes, only a few cycles per second apart, their independent use determined by association with the lead-in note. Worse than this, the practice of changing keys, known as modulation, is practically impossible because the sequence of scale steps just doesn't jibe. To a singer, this presented little problem because instant adjustment could be made. But to a piano maker, it was a mess. The notes that didn't sound right earned the name of 'woof tones.'

"A system called 'mean tone temperament' came along about 1500 which solved some of the problems by making the two larger steps the same size. But modulation through all of the keys still remained a problem. In 1690, Andreas Werkmeister invented the system that is used today called 'equal temperament.' This system juggled the size of all three steps around until the two large steps were equal in size, and the smaller semi-tone was exactly half the size of the established large step.

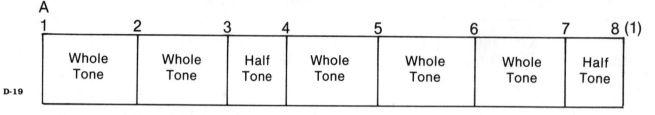

D-19

ESTABLISHMENT OF THE CHROMATIC SCALE

"The discovery of equal temperament ushered in the establishment of the chromatic scale. The chromatic scale divides the octave up into twelve equal semi-tones or half-steps, comparable to the distance of one fret on the guitar. The interval between each half-step is the ratio 1.059. A whole step is two half-steps, or a two fret distance. The chromatic is the master scale from which all other scales we use are derived. Along with the ability to build chords, equal temperament allowed a musician to play in any of twelve different keys without modulation problems. Choosing a key means centering your number one tonic note on one of the twelve chromatic notes that divide any octave and building your scale with a chosen interval pattern above this point using whole or half-steps. Bach wrote *The Well Tempered Clavichord* in 1722 to show the universal applications of equal temperament. This novel piece modulates around the twelve tonic centers, one by one, until all possible keys have been employed.

"Now let's stand back and take a look, Boy. First we have ten octaves in the range of human hearing. Then we divide the octave into twelve equal parts called half-steps with two half-steps making a whole step. Starting on the tonic note, the major scale in any key will have the following interval pattern.

Whole Whole Half Whole Whole Whole Half

D-20

"The piano is set up to play the major scale in the key of C using only white notes. The key of C is also the base from which the alphabet names were assigned to the seven major scale degrees. It is a curious thing why they didn't center things around the letter A, but they didn't. So here is what you've got:

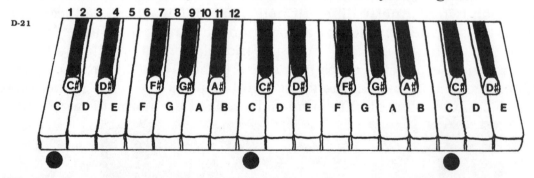

D-21

"Everything is originally based on a 440 A note. Using equal temperament, we can figure out the C note below this A note and call it middle C. It is from this centrally located C note that the alphabet letter note names take their start and continue with every white key getting an alphabet letter between A and G. As we have seen, a major scale is not an evenly runged ladder. So in order to take up the slack, the five black notes of the piano play the five passed over half-steps between the major intervals that are whole steps. This results in the white keys E and F, and also B and C being directly next to each other. Now, let's expand our view to take in all of the octaves of the piano.

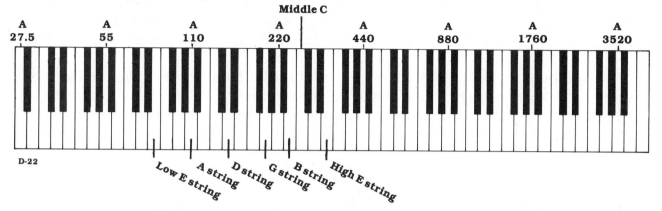

"The common system of written music employs the alphabet note system using the key of C as a base. The five line staff has one major scale degree from the key of C on or between each line of the staff. These can be altered chromatically by the addition of a sharp or flat symbol on a line or space of the note to be altered. This is how music written in other keys, or the use of scales other than the major are transcribed. Here are the two most common staffs with all of the notes from the major scale in C. Middle C, which marks the center of our range between high and low, falls on a ledger line between staffs. For use with the piano, the upper staff, which uses the treble clef, is generally for use with the right hand. The lower staff has the bass clef symbol and is usually played with the left hand. Those notes with squares around them are the open strings of the six string guitar."

The old man took a key out of his pocket and walked to the front door of the house. Unlocking it and stepping in, the boy followed in amazement. "You must have dozens of guitars here, Old Man," the boy said with wide-eyed words, as he surveyed the living room.

"What can I say, Boy, except the piano and the amps are in the other room."

From top to bottom, the walls and floors were full of every conceivable musical instrument and accessory. The boy really had to wonder about the old man at this point. What was this all about? How could an old man on the tracks have a set-up like this? "This place is like a music store, Old Man."

The old man took it all in with a smile and said, "Music house. Please, Boy, get your terminology straight. Now don't be overcome by the material abundance. Remember, all of these instruments can be difficult to play at times. Don't think me rich or poor, Boy. Just sit down on the couch for a minute, listen to me play the blues, and meditate on the range we live."

The old man sat across the room and immediately sounded an old slow blues. It was like the tempo had been going all the time and the old man just tuned into it like a radio. After three times through the changes, the old man nodded his head in the direction of the couch, and the boy drifted off into sleep.

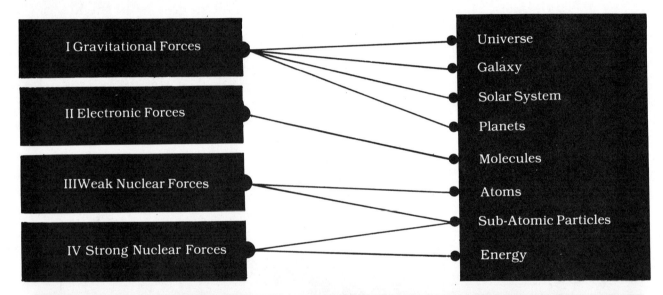

5. Major Breakdown

hange is going to go on, Boy. So now we change from looking at the dry background information that establishes your base of knowledge, to actually working the board with your hand. Big change. You ready, Boy?"

The boy slowly opened one eye to see the old man in the same chair playing the same guitar. The events of the day before flashed through his mind at high speed. The frustrations that drove him out of the city resurfaced in his thoughts. It was the desire to learn that made the whole thing happen. He never would have left his parents' house if it weren't for that. Maybe the boy didn't know it directly, but the core of his intention was to learn how to play. After several hours of sleep, he sat up quickly and spoke directly to the old man. "I want to learn how to play blues — *fast!* I don't want to wait."

"Doesn't take you long to wake up, Boy. I like that. Well then, let me talk. The desire to want to learn is essential, but does not bake the cake with its own power. You have to let your desire yield to that frame of mind where you say to yourself, ok, this is it. The time is now for this. I will do this one thing until I understand by doing it myself. Cross over that line and make the thing come right up in front of your nose and say, 'Here it is.' "

The boy had slept away the day and the sun was low in the sky and the air across the fields was clear and dry. "Now look out that window to the edge of that field. Now look at the wall across the room. Then hold the tip of your index finger in front of your eyes and look at the skin that makes your finger print. The last frame is the one I want you to get down. When you have any doubts, get out the pencil and paper and work things out. Take your fretboard and hold it right up to your eyes and stare at it for half an hour if that is what it takes. Don't think of it as work — just dive in. Put in the time, and you will learn fast.

"I have seen a lot of students get as far as you are now and then stop because of the demand upon the beginner to learn different concepts before he can really get down to playing. Just believe that it will all add up in the end, and try to be patient as I take up one related subject at a time. Let's go ahead with it. The word scale comes from the Latin 'scala' which means ladder. Before you slept, you learned how the twelve-step chromatic scale is an equal breakdown of the octave into twelve steps. We call the chromatic a scale, and it is. But it is easier to see it as the complete ladder with every rung. Here is the chromatic scale in the key of E along the low E string enumerated with both number and alphabet letters signifying individual scale degrees.

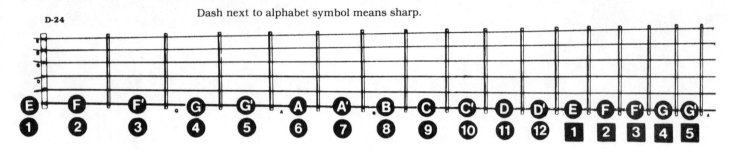

Dash next to alphabet symbol means sharp.

D-24

INTERVALS

"An interval is the difference in pitch between two notes. There are two different kinds of intervals, *melodic* if the tones are sounded successively, and *harmonic* if the tones are sounded simultaneously. We already know that the smallest common interval is the half step, which is the distance between any two degrees of the chromatic scale. The whole step is two of these degrees. Just look at this one more time and then we'll have our terms straight and I won't tell you again.

Semi-tone = Half-tone = Half-step = 1 chromatic scale degree = one fret distance

Whole tone = Whole step = 2 chromatic scale degrees = 2 fret distances

"We can now use these terms to give an interval pattern for a specific scale. This will tell us which of the twelve chromatic degrees we might choose to make any scale. Let's take a look at the major scale as it works out on the low E string.

"Please note that the Major scale degrees are given by number. Usually, when a reference is given to a numbered scale degree it is in reference to the numbered scale degrees of the major scale and not the chromatic. For instance, 'the third' of the major scale in E is the G sharp note. You will find all sorts of reference to the degrees of the major for building chords or working out melody lines. The trick is to just skip over the irregular chromatic interval pattern that makes up the major scale and consider only the notes that are in the major scale, giving each one the same value as you go. A system for interval values exists which uses the major scale degrees as its base.

"For the sake of quick understanding, I will group the categories of interval terminology into three parts.

● 1.   The most common way for informal guitarists to state an interval is to just say the number of frets between two notes on a given string. You know, 'go up five frets and do this.' You can also state the number of chromatic steps between the two points or specify an interval by using the terms whole-step or half-step.

● 2.   The second way refers directly to the number of major scale degrees involved in a given interval. Using this terminology, a second is the distance between any two scale degrees immediately beside each other in the major scale. Now think about this for awhile, and you will see that 'a second' above the 'Do' first of the scale is the 'Re' note. This is two frets.

Now consider 'a second' above the third or seventh degree and you will find this to be one fret. So, what's going on? When we use the term with just one word describing the interval, for example, 'a fifth' above the second is the seventh, we mean go up that many degrees starting from the one you're on, counted as one. Doesn't have anything to do with the chromatic, Boy. Numbers higher than seven are in reference to the major degrees in the next higher octave. The eighth is the tonic first again, and the ninth is really the second — but double the frequency, remember?

●3.   The third way uses a two-word system to account for the distance in chromatic steps, still working within a major scale reference. This has to do with the irregularity I pointed out in the size interval between major scale degrees. Apparently it causes a big hassle in how they figure out how far things are apart from each other in the chromatic scale. So, they worked out this involved system to account for all the possibilities by calling the various intervals either major, minor, perfect, augmented, or diminished. [Appendix 4].

"This may or may not seem like a lot of mumbo-jumbo to you, Boy. Just know the degrees of the chromatic scale and the major scale and be able to distinguish between them. Get used to them and you will be alright. I'll usually call the number of frets for changes up and down the board. There is a twist you can get caught in that I should point out. 'A fourth' is a term that usually means to count up three more degrees and that's the interval in the major that you want. A reference to 'the fourth' means that you are to deal with the fourth, called 'fa' as a particular degree center.

"A *simple* interval is smaller than an octave in its size while a *compound* interval is larger than an octave. Two intervals *complement* each other if they add up to a complete octave. Using other words, one interval is the inversion of the other if together they make one octave.

MAJOR DEGREES

"Well, you know the distance between the steps, but how much do you actually know about the steps themselves? Of course the tonic is the first stake you drive in the ground saying, 'I'm going to use this octave for a reference starting at this point.' The tonic is the root note. Once one note has been played, people who have good *relative* pitch can identify the correct pitch of other notes. People who have *absolute* pitch can judge the pitch of any note, even if no other reference notes have been sounded.

"The second is two frets up from the first and is called the supertonic. The mediant is located four frets up from the tonic and is usually called the third. The fourth is a half-step up from the third, and is called the sub-dominant. The fifth is the dominant and is named according to its use and influence. Incidently, the sub-dominant takes its name from being a fifth below the tonic, not because it is immediately under the dominant in the scale. The sixth is the sub-mediant and the seventh is the leading tone, so called because of the tendency to draw into the tonic center from the seventh position.

"All of these notes are in the family. You should get to know each one at a time because, really Boy, you will be on your own with the guitar the rest of your life. These things won't change and the whole of music theory is built on these degrees in one way or another.

"Any notes an octave apart are said to be in perfect *consonance*. This means that they are generally understood to sound like they were meant to be together and do not clash harmonically when played. All major scale degrees should first be compared to the tonic. Try this one:

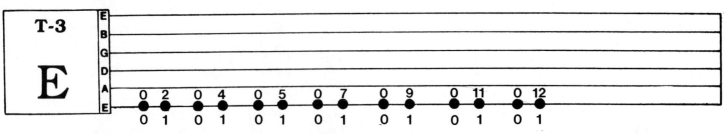

"The relationship between the notes themselves is a life-long study. In relation to the tonic, it is generally understood that the third, the fifth and the sixth are thought of as consonant, whereas the second, fourth and seventh create a sort of dissonance. This disturbance causes tension which tends to resolve itself toward notes which are in consonance. This is really what blues lead guitar is all about — a back and forth sway of tension, suspension/resolve, and relief, which is dictated not by the notes themselves, but by the performer's use of them. Sorry to give you one jelly bean and then put the bag away. I never said that it was going to be easy.

"Let's go down on the board. First off, we know that the major scale on the low E string for the key of E looks like this:

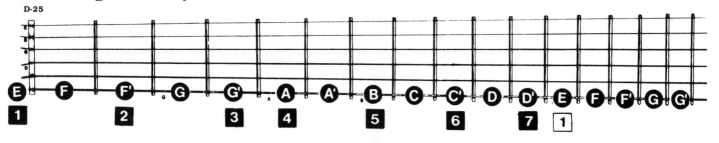

" For the sake of thoroughness, I want you to see the chromatic scale on the whole board across all six strings, up to the thirteenth fret.

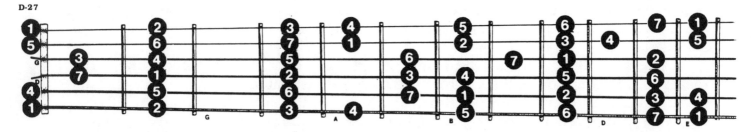

"Now, picking only the degrees of the major out of the chromatic, the resulting pattern for the major scale in E is this mess:

"The only way to make sense of this is to take a quick look at how much the human hand can accommodate and then subdivide our pattern accordingly.

FINGERING PRINCIPLES

"The most basic of all fingering is the one fret per finger climb. Start by placing the index finger on the low E string at the first fret, playing an F note, climb up the chromatic scale one degree at a time until you get to the pinky at the fourth fret. Repeat process on all six strings.

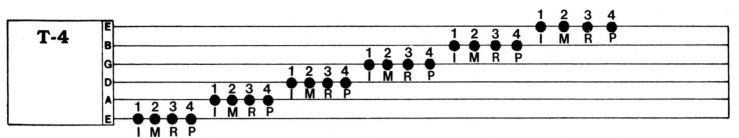

"The only thing that I want to add at this time to this basic method is the technique of using the outside fingers, the index and the pinky, to pick up an extra note a half-step above or below their prescribed position. Don't cheat by sliding the note. Lift it clear over the fret, press the string firmly, and pick it.

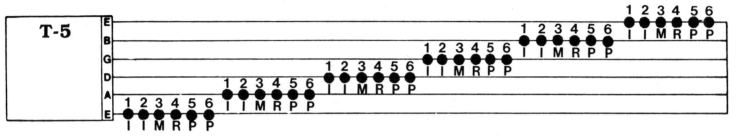

"So now you have one finger per fret and an extra note for the pinky and index. This makes a really great warm-up exercise. I am going to teach you the proper way to finger your way through the major scale now. Don't get discouraged, but know that it is going to hurt your hand a little because of muscle tension. When this happens, stop and shake some blood into the hand. Work it out by making a fist and then opening your hand wide with the fingers spread out.

MAJOR SCALE CLIMBING IN E

"I am going to tell you something very important now, so please listen closely. All scales — it doesn't matter which ones — leave a twelve fret repeating pattern on the fretboard. This is because of the length of the chromatic scale. But get it in your head that the tonic has to appear someplace on the low E string and this is the place where you will go to get centered. Our present example is in the key of E, so look for the whole territory — twelve frets long and six strings wide — to start to repeat itself on the twelfth fret, because it does. The breakdown that follows from this point will show you the complexities that a twelve-fret pattern can present. Just stick with me once all the way through. That is all I ask. No, you don't need to know all of these positions in order to be a great blues guitarist, but I did go to all the trouble to work them out correctly for you. Aren't you interested?

The boy was chomping at the bit, sitting up straight, tuning his guitar, running chromatic exercises to limber up. "Now understand one or two things about these before you tear into them, Boy. First off, they always start and end on a tonic E note and ascend through the major scale one degree at a time. Secondly, they have been worked out carefully according to what finger plays what fret, so read it, and play it. Thirdly, each covers a part of the twelve-fret territory, so be aware of what part you are using in the overall picture. On this first one, you start with the low E open. Now when you go to play 'Re,' your first impulse is to play it with the index, but use the middle because you will use the index for notes across the first fret. It ends on the high E string open. You can play one or the other of the boxed notes. Ready, Boy?

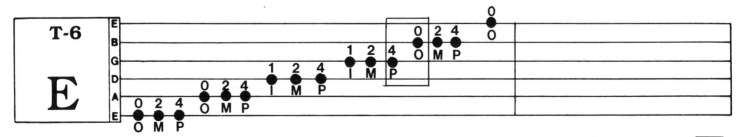

"I'm going to start you this time with the index centering on the second fret. It's one fret per finger all the way up to the sixth fret on the fifth string which extends the pinky's range to its fullest. It ends on the E note on the second string at the fifth fret.

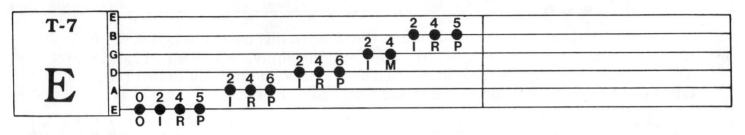

"This next position opens with the octave of the open low E played on the fifth string at the seventh fret. Now listen, this position plays the same note as the tonic on the second fret of the D or fourth string. You can always find the tonic here. This passage will show you how to step through the territory defined by the major below a line across the seventh fret. This is where you lock in the pinky to start it off. It's one finger per, from there down. This fingering of the scale ends on a logical climb to the tonic on the high E. Get ready for a transitory move with the index up to the ninth fret from the fourth.

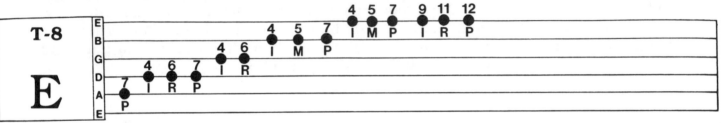

"The next one covers the ground from the seventh fret up, centering the first note with the index on the tonic E, fifth string, seventh fret. Get ready for the index to do its trick again on the high E. This time it's just the index up a whole step. Climb it up to the tonic the same as last time.

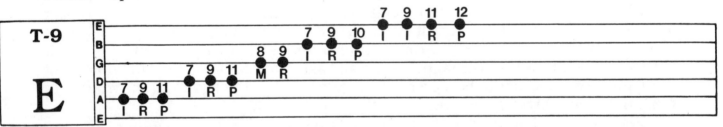

"This next time through starts with the same actual note played by the previous arrangement, but the note's position is on the low E string twelfth fret, yet another octave mark. Now understand, here are three positions that play an identically pitched E note: sixth string/twelfth fret, fifth string/seventh fret, and third string/second fret.

"Tough move on the fourth string comes when pinky has to go the distance to the thirteenth fret. Ends across the same fret that it started on, exactly two octaves above its opening note.

"Here is a difficult but efficient way to finger the E major scale on and above the twelfth fret which contains two tonic E notes on the outside strings. The bottom two strings are taken up in whole steps. When you play the fourth string, come down with the middle finger to play the seventh of the scale, then ring the tonic at fourteen. Notice the either/or box. Ends with the index on the twelfth fret, first string.

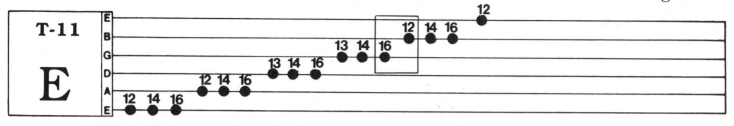

"Here's one for later, Boy. Try to go through the second approach but in the octave position centering the index on the fourteenth fret, rather than the second. The first note of the second approach is an easy open string, but the challenge here is to play the E at the twelfth fret with the index and then move up a whole step to center on fourteen. Everything else remains the same except that it is twelve frets higher."

"Am I supposed to remember all this, Old Man?" the boy asked shaking his hand. "Hey, I didn't design the instrument, Boy. Just follow me through this next phase and worry about it later."

MAJOR SCALE CLIMBING IN A MAJOR

"Back to the board. Here are two diagrams showing the major scale in the key of A only on the fifth string and then on the whole board. Know that the interval pattern for the major scale degrees stays the same. It is just that we are now establishing the tonic on the open low A, or fifth string.

D-28

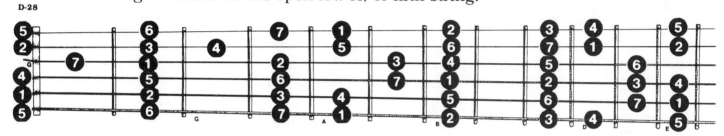

"As you will come to know by experience, each key has its advantages and disadvantages. You will find certain A tonic centers to regularly appear exactly five half-steps above where you know them to be in E. Look up and down, then across. In A you can play the fifth, sixth and seventh of the scale, starting on the low E string open, before you work up to the tonic A note on the same string. The same thing is true on the high E string which has the same pattern.

"The fifth string beckons with its open A note. We will now center our tonic at this note and set out into uncharted territory just like we did with the key of E.

"The first way I'll show you starts with the open A string and climbs the ladder right up to the fifth fret on the first string. Notice the either/or box.

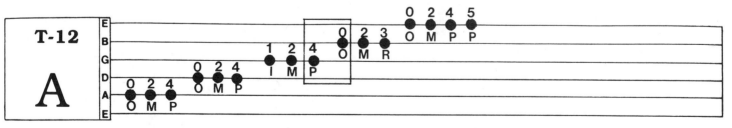

"The next one has an optional opening tonic note using either the open A string or the sixth string, fifth fret A note. Either way you go, you center the index on the second fret and wind up on the fifth fret, playing the tonic with the pinky on the thinnest string.

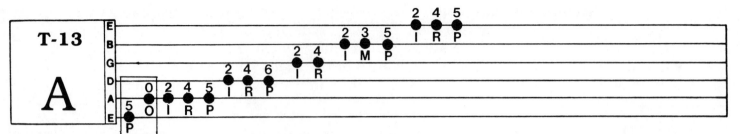

"We're moving on up, so get ready to center the index across the fifth fret where A notes are on the E strings. Pinky is extended to its full range to get notes on the ninth fret. Ends on an easy index at the root note tonic, first string, fifth fret.

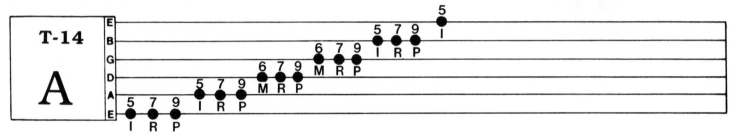

"The next way starts with a jump by the index finger of two frets from the fifth fret to the seventh where it stays positioned across all six. Ends up on the second string with the pinky playing tonic A at the tenth fret."

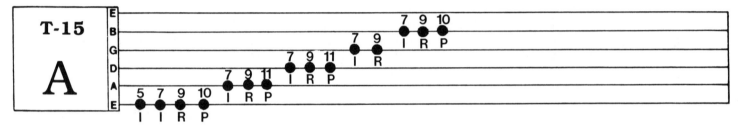

"Let's look at the last two together. They both begin and end on the same note, however, the first one begins with the pinky and works the area directly on and below the twelfth fret. The second way centers the index along this double dot twelfth fret and then walks you up to sweet seventeen on the high E. This is the highest A note that you can play on the guitar."

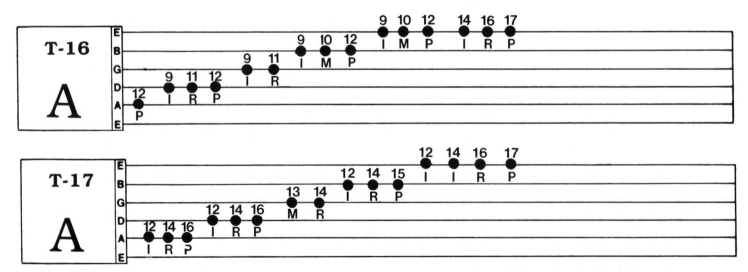

The old man started in directly, "Now I want to show you." But he never got to finish his sentence.

"Hold on, Old Man!" the boy said as he shuffled his papers. The boy stood up and walked toward the next room, picking up a guitar along the way. "See you in an hour, Old Man."

6. Chords From Scales

fter an hour, the old man walked into the next room to see the boy. "Hey, Boy. That 'Do, Re, Mi' stuff is going to drive me crazy. Don't you know anything else?" The boy looked up to see if the old man meant what he said. "Now that I have your attention, Boy, I have to tell you how proud I am that you have practiced your scales. Talk is sometimes necessary to convey concepts, but nothing gets it like playing. To get familiar with the notes, that is the goal. After that, the words reinforce what you discover while practicing. Disciplined scale climbing is gold, Boy. That quiet hour of practice — I'm glad you know. We don't know *how* the mind gets to know something, and we don't need to know. What we need to realize is that repetitive study will impress the mind. Running the scales is the only way I know for a student to arrive at that point where the jive is 'second nature.' "

"I'm beginning to feel it, Old Man. My hand cramped up at first, but after awhile, I got my second wind and was able to get above it. It seemed like too much information when we first went over it. But after practicing, I can see how finite the system really is."

"Finite in element, but infinitely variable." The boy knew it was time to listen, because the old man was walking in circles again, seemingly staring through the walls. "Chords are next. Two points one octave apart, twelve equal steps between them, the major a selection of seven of these twelve. You have been playing these steps melodically, but what if we chose certain steps from the major and play them harmonically. Then we have chords.

"Chords are the simultaneous sounding of three or more tones. Two tones played simultaneously are called an interval. When two tones are sounded together, the ear sometimes hears a false tone that is of a proportional frequency to the original tones. If two notes are played together and the volume of one increases to where the other cannot be heard, the quieter tone is said to be masked. The consequence of playing three or more notes at once can get complicated, but as usual, there is a strict formula that we can use to get a start.

TRIADS

"This formula is for the triad, which consists of a fundamental note, its upper third, and its upper fifth. In other terms it may be called two superimposed intervals of a third above a fundamental. Things get thick pretty fast when we ask the question, 'What kind of third?' Using different combinations of the major third, that's four frets, and the minor third, that's three frets, we come up with four species of triads:

The major triad consists of a major third and a minor third,
The minor triad consists of a minor third and a major third,
The augmented triad consists of two major thirds,
The diminished triad consists of two minor thirds.

"All that you have to do to make a major chord is to take a note, call it 'Do' then go up to 'Mi' and 'Sol' and you have the big three. This process is called 'building' a triad above a note, and unless otherwise noted, it will mean to construct a major chord above a given note. Now, don't get mixed up about key. You can sing 'Do, Re, Mi' then you can build triads above each of these notes individually using them as fundamental note centers for building. In the key of C, 'Do, Re and Mi' are C, D and E notes. If we build traids above these three points, the result would be three chords — C major, D major and E major. The three notes these chords were built on still remain as the first, second and third scale degrees in the key of A. The processes remain independent. Of course, the word 'building' is just a term. We will more than likely just play the chords we need in various positions, having known the basic configuration which results from building.

"The minor triad is the same as the major with the exception of the third degree, which is diminished one half-step. So you take the major chord, keep it as it is, but take the third of the scale and move it down one fret. The major and minor are the two basic chords from which practically all others are built. Before we go on to other chords, let's paint the picture of how the E major chord is constructed. We start with the chromatic scale below the fifth fret. This shows all of the notes that there are on the board below this point. Next I will show you all of the major scale degrees below the fourth fret. Then we highlight only the first, third and the fifth of the scale below the third fret.

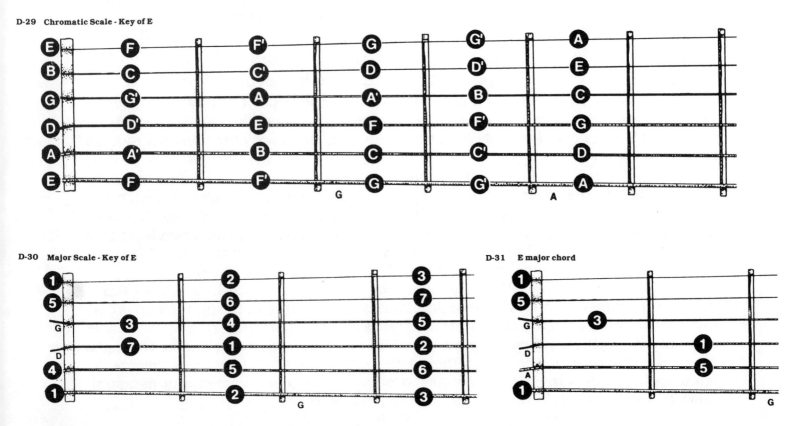

D-29 Chromatic Scale - Key of E

D-30 Major Scale - Key of E

D-31 E major chord

"Do you see how we draw the chord out of the other degrees? Now if we take the [...]nor chord.

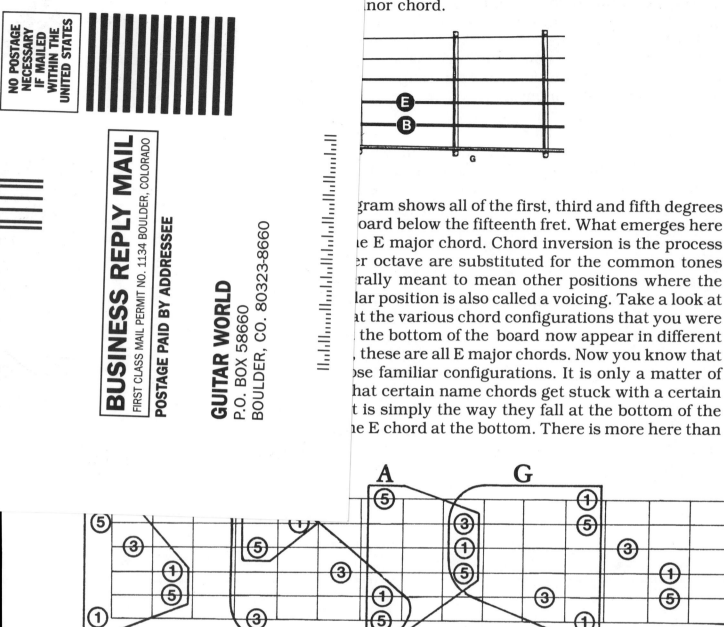

[...]gram shows all of the first, third and fifth degrees [...]oard below the fifteenth fret. What emerges here [...]e E major chord. Chord inversion is the process [...]er octave are substituted for the common tones [...]rally meant to mean other positions where the [...]lar position is also called a voicing. Take a look at [...]t the various chord configurations that you were [...] the bottom of the board now appear in different [...], these are all E major chords. Now you know that [...]se familiar configurations. It is only a matter of [...]hat certain name chords get stuck with a certain [...]t is simply the way they fall at the bottom of the [...]e E chord at the bottom. There is more here than

"Now gear up and get this. Do you see how the pattern of E chord intervals from the last diagram repeats every twelve frets? It is the same game as all repeating scale patterns: twelve frets high and six strings wide. How could it be any different? It is the same pattern that you have been fingering for the past hour with the second, fourth, sixth and seventh removed. The twelve-note chromatic covers the board, then we choose our interval pattern, or simply the notes we want from one octave. Then we run that pattern up and down all six strings, box it off into something you can use, and . . . that's the picture. How do you think I make these diagrams, anyway?

OTHER CHORDS

"Now that you know how the major and minor are made, I'm going to give you the basis behind a few more chords and then pull out. You can go to music school and stay in the music library for years and still not know everything about chords. The blues guitarist deals basically with the major, the seventh, and the minor chord occasionally. But don't uncork the champagne because acquiring a *working* knowledge of the major is a full-time job. You can play one, two, three, four, five or six of the notes at once. You can strum them up, down, or alternately. You can play a chord in a quick swish or in a broken arpeggio. You can use one chord for rhythm or build chords on the notes of the melody line, or run any number of scales over the known chord configuration. Another thing — the major E chord inversion diagram we looked at is only for one major chord. Yes, it is the same for all major chords, but every time the song goes to a new chord, your head has some switching to do." The boy slid down in his chair.

"It's okay, Boy. You learn by doing, anyway. Now we have our major and minor chords, and to these we can add other scale degrees from the major and get other chords. The chord we commonly call the seventh is actually the major chord with the flatted seventh added above the fifth. The chord with the actual seventh is called the major seventh chord.

"Chords that have numbers higher than seven in their call numbers are generally understood to have the flatted seventh included. Such is the case for the ninth chord which has a line up like this: 1st, 3rd, 5th, 7th (flatted), and 9th. A lot of chords just add scale degrees, some of which are chromatically altered, to the major chord line up. These have names like 'the added sixth chord.'

"When a fourth is added to a major or minor triad, it is called 'suspended.' These are used as tap-ons in the blues and come into play because of the important relationship between the first and the fourth. I made up a chord chart for you which includes all of the chords that I think you will find used in a blues format. I want you to just keep it loose in your guitar case for reference. But make sure to go over each chord a few times to understand what is going on, because sometimes the same chord has a few different fingerings. We will start with the E-based chords which take their names from that low E string tonic, then we move onto A, B and others."

Chord Chart

O = Open
X = Don't play or mute

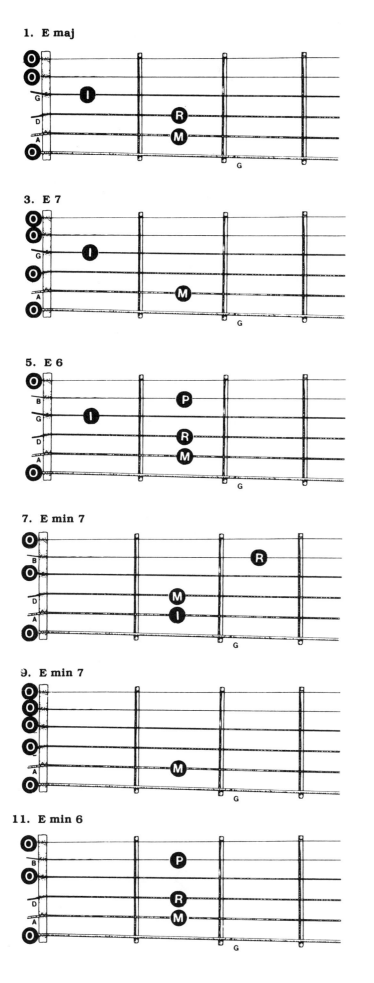

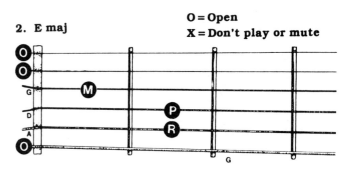

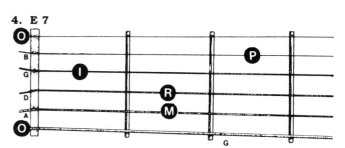

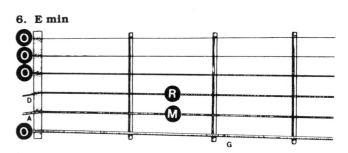

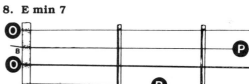

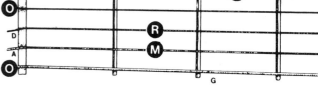

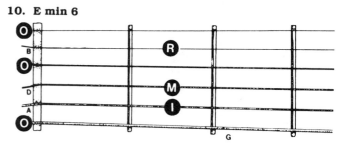

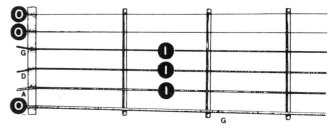

49

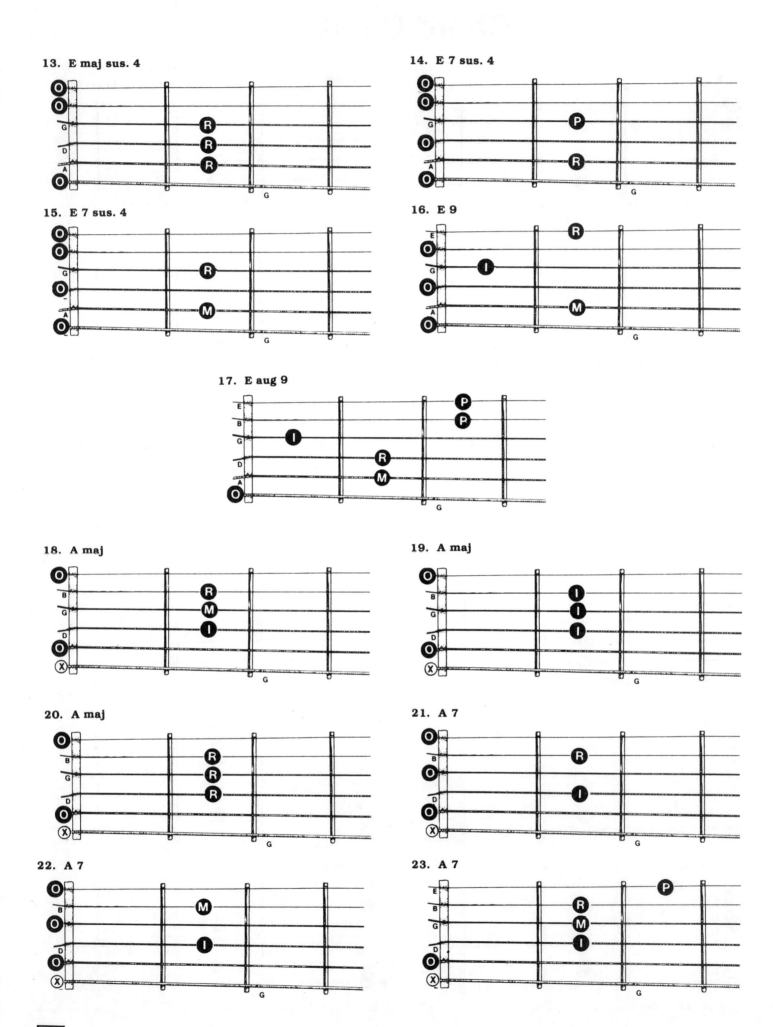

24. A 7

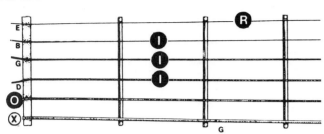

25. A 6

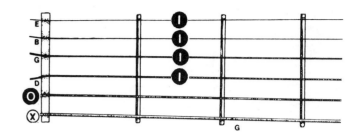

26. A min

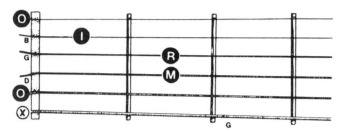

27. A min

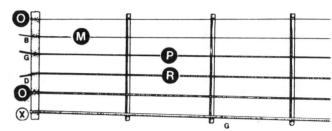

28. A min 7

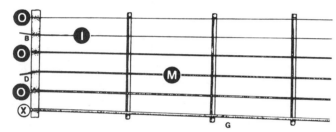

29. A min 7

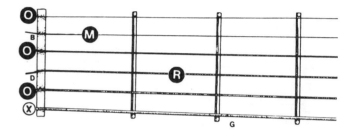

30. A min 7

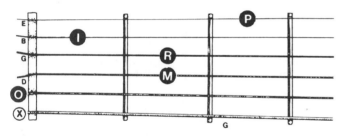

31. A min 6

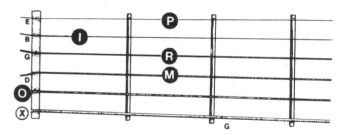

32. A maj sus 4

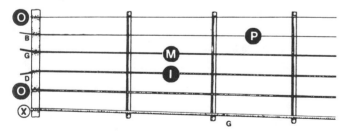

33. A maj sus 4

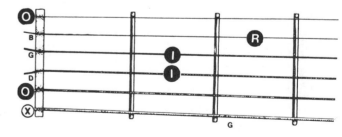

34. A 7 sus 4

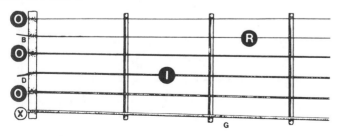

35. A maj 7

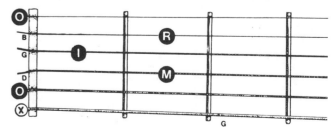

36. B maj

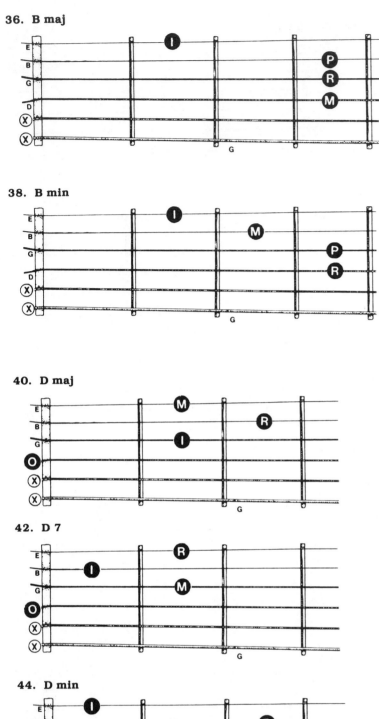

37. B 7

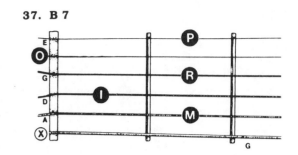

38. B min

39. B 9

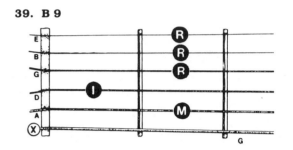

40. D maj

41. D maj

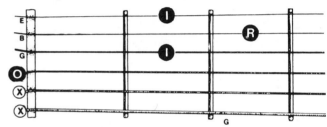

42. D 7

43. D 6

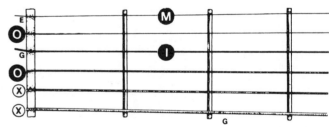

44. D min

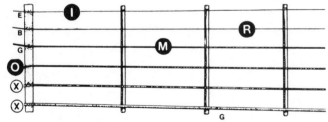

45. D min 7

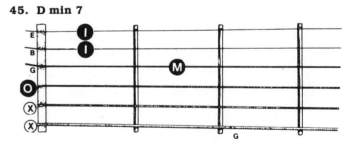

46. D min 6

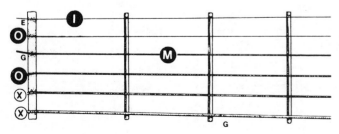

47. D maj 7

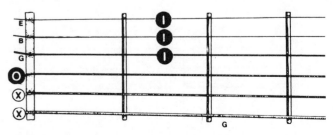

48. C maj

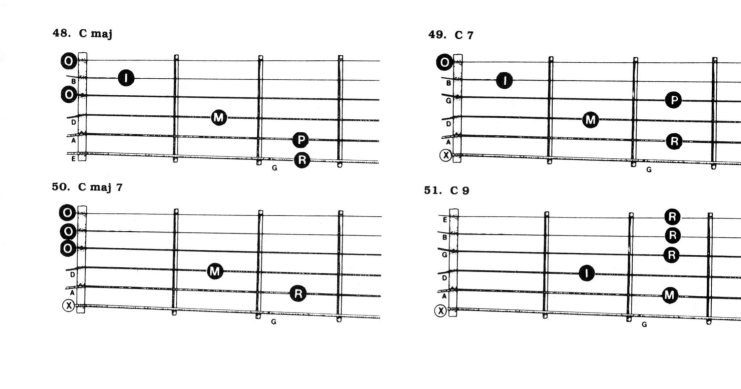

49. C 7

50. C maj 7

51. C 9

52. G maj

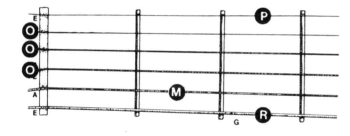

53. G maj

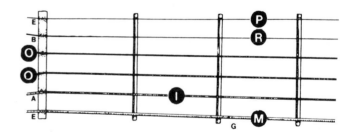

54. G 7

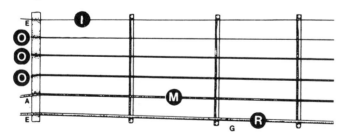

55. G min 7

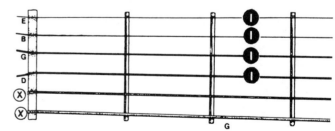

56. G maj 7

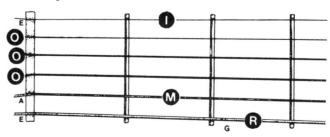

BAR CHORDS

"Bar chords are movable chord configurations which can be variably positioned up and down the fretboard to accomodate different tonic centers. In the case of the major E chord, the primary chord for the guitar, you study the series of E-based chords which were just presented, and then think in terms of moving them up the board. This is usually done by putting the index finger across all six strings to replace the nut that accepts the strings at the end of the fingerboard. The last three fingers of the hand are used to make the chord immediately above the bar. Because the E chord takes its name from the low E string played open, the E chord bar series has a sixth string root base. This means that the tonic center of the movable bar chord series will take its name from the note played by the index finger on the low E string.

"One thing is for sure, you have to know the letter name notes for every note on the low E string up and down, inside and out. If you bar the E chord to the first fret, you have an F chord. Barred to the fifth fret, you will have an A chord. Let's look at the E bar chord series positioned at the fifth fret. This will make it a study of A chords, but movable is the word. You are free to move the whole cookie cutter pattern to any fret, name the tonic after the note played on the E string, then you have the root name of the series. One nice thing about bar chords is the fact that you only have to study the system for one major chord, then you just move that up and down. All basic open chords played at the bottom of the guitar are movable. However, it is the E and A major series that are used most of the time because of their simple, compact design and their optimal open positions.

"The A bar series works on the same principles as the E bar chords except they have a fifth string root. They will take their tonic name from the note played on the fifth string by the index finger. Although the E note is the fifth of the A scale, and a primary chord component, it is preferable not to play the E string when making the A bar. Give the priority to the tonic played by the index finger on the fifth string and mute the sixth with the very tip of the index."

E bar chords at fifth fret -- Sixth string root.

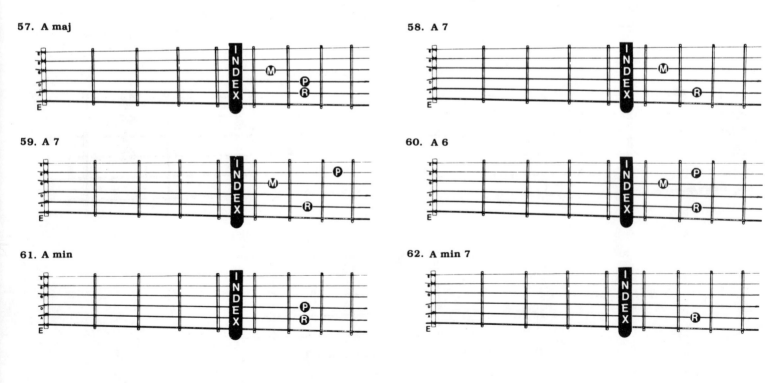

57. A maj

58. A 7

59. A 7

60. A 6

61. A min

62. A min 7

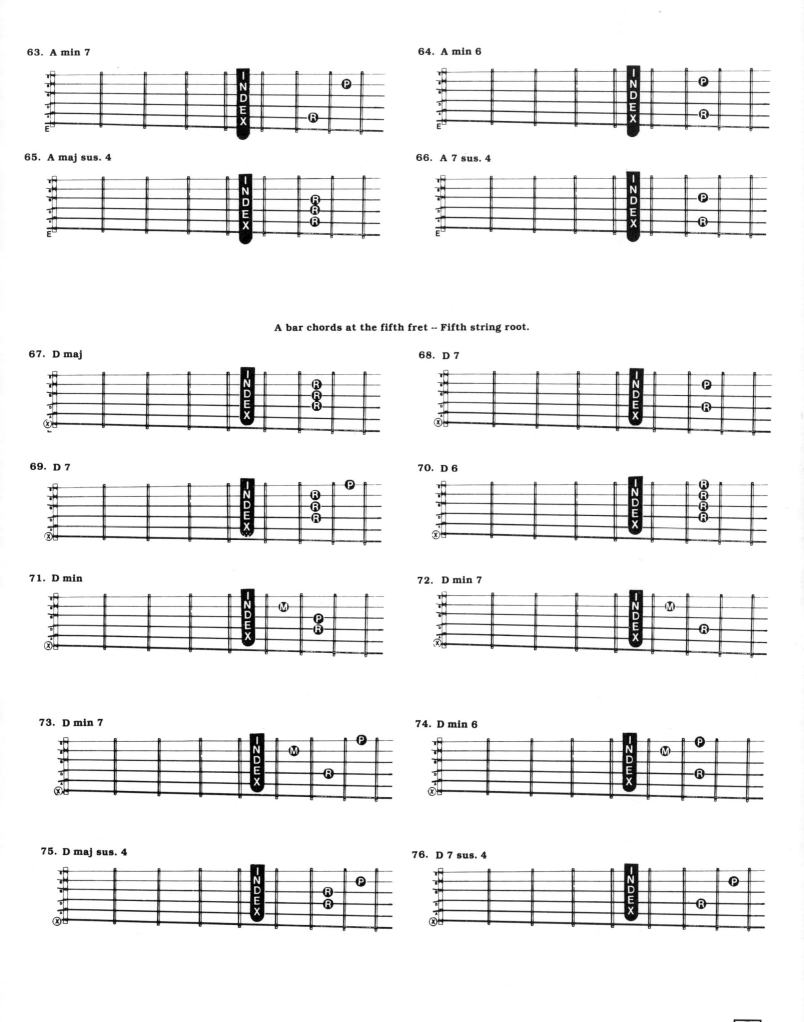

63. A min 7

64. A min 6

65. A maj sus. 4

66. A 7 sus. 4

A bar chords at the fifth fret -- Fifth string root.

67. D maj

68. D 7

69. D 7

70. D 6

71. D min

72. D min 7

73. D min 7

74. D min 6

75. D maj sus. 4

76. D 7 sus. 4

OTHER MOVABLES

"The more you stare at it, the more you will know. That goes for watching other guitarists, too, because you will be surprised how fast you can learn tricks if you just watch closely and piece it together. Here is a movables series of chords based on the C 7th chord (number 49). I will show it to you twice — once in its simplest position and again with added-on notes. The chord on the left is a movable seventh pattern with a fifth string root. The note played on the fifth string is the tonic with the third and seventh following. This chord is great for blues in both A or E because it is easy to reach from the E chord bar which centers on the sixth string. It is also useful for playing a B chord, centering out of that note on the second fret, fifth string. The chord on the right is really the same guy with notes played on the two high strings at the fifth fret. The B string plays a ninth of the root, while the high E plays the fifth. Please note the alternate fingering for these two strings. These chords can easily slide up and down as a unit.

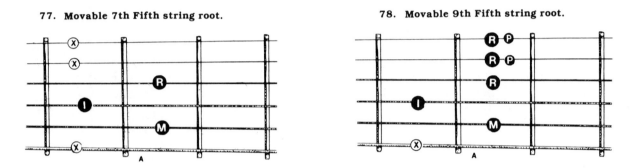

77. Movable 7th Fifth string root.   78. Movable 9th Fifth string root.

"The next two chords are the same movable seventh chord but on the low E string. Move them around and up and down. Get the feel for sliding the finger together up to the desired fret. Pinky is optional and plays the same note as the index.

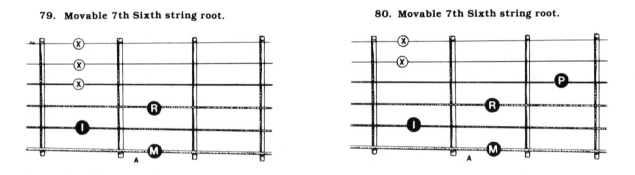

79. Movable 7th Sixth string root.   80. Movable 7th Sixth string root.

CHORDS COMMON TO KEY

"Let's see now, Boy. You know all about what chords are, but you don't know which ones to use for what. This brings us back to the major scale degrees. Here is the story in a nutshell — the basic chords that you will need to play the blues are the three major triads built on the first, fourth and fifth of the major scale. For the key of E, that is the E major, the A major, and the B major chord. If you are ever at a complete loss, just count up five and seven frets directly above the tonic and you will have the three chord centers that you need. For now, I want you to KNOW WHICH CHORDS YOU WILL NEED. Position and sequence will come a little later.

"The three basic chords used in the key of A are A major, D major and E major. These are the pillars that hold up the blues changes, Boy, so you better know them!

Here are two charts that show the position of the first, the fourth, and the fifth in both of our home keys:

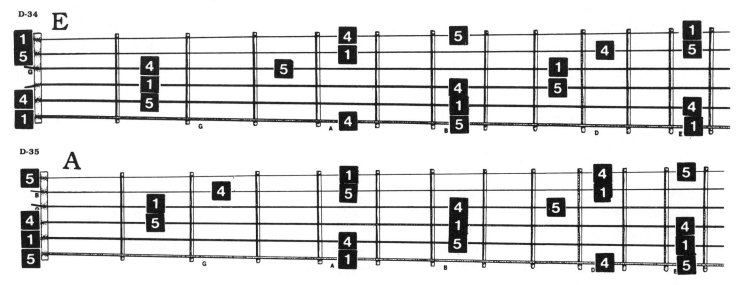

"Another chord that is useful in blues chording, and often found in rock, is the major chord located a whole step below the tonic. For the key of A, this is a G major chord, and for E it is a D chord. This guy is used in turnarounds which simply go around like a wheel. An example of this is the chord sequence E, D, A, E in the key of E.

"To finish the chord picture, we will take a quick look at Relative minor chords. Every major chord has a relative minor chord which takes its position *three frets below the major chord in the form of a minor.* This means the introduction of three more chords for use in each key — one for each of the first, the fourth and the fifth. We will see this 'three frets down' relative step again very soon when we go into lead guitar. The relative minor chords are not widely used in blues, but do appear widely in popular songs and the slower, more melodic blues-based ballads.

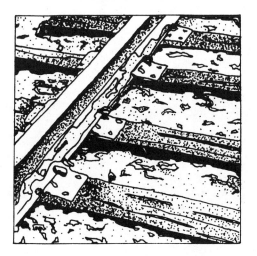

"Let's go and sit at the kitchen table, Boy, and drink some beer," the old man said as he walked for the door with the boy in tow. They had talked the sun down again, and the night air was cool as it drifted in the open windows.

"Isn't it funny, Boy, how things go when you study real hard? It feels like you're cutting everything else out. But it is really not that at all. It makes you sharper for any endeavor. So it's good for you in the end."

"What is next, Old Man. Only you know."

"Well, we have come a long way already. I know that it is not easy studying basic guitar when you want to move on, but please have patience. We can get on to the blues form, now."

The boy felt he had earned his position. The old man started to draw lines on some clean paper while the night train rolled its rhythms over the fields and into the woods.

The boy gazed out the window at the fine spot of white light made by the distant train. "Let's go out and meet the train, Old Man." The old man gently set his beer down on the middle of the table.

"Come back now, Boy. You've lost your edge. You say that you want to learn about guitar technique. Well, there are techniques in studying the guitar as well. The longer you hold the water gate at the top of the dam, the higher the water gets, resulting in a huge lake behind the dam with miles and miles of coastline. Deep water, Boy!

"So, have one beer and slip back into the first phase, Boy. You're back out at the edge of the field. Remember, look at your fingertips. Don't worry, Boy. We'll have two beers and a sip of whiskey the night we jump the train."

The boy looked up from his fingertips to see the old man gazing out to the rails.

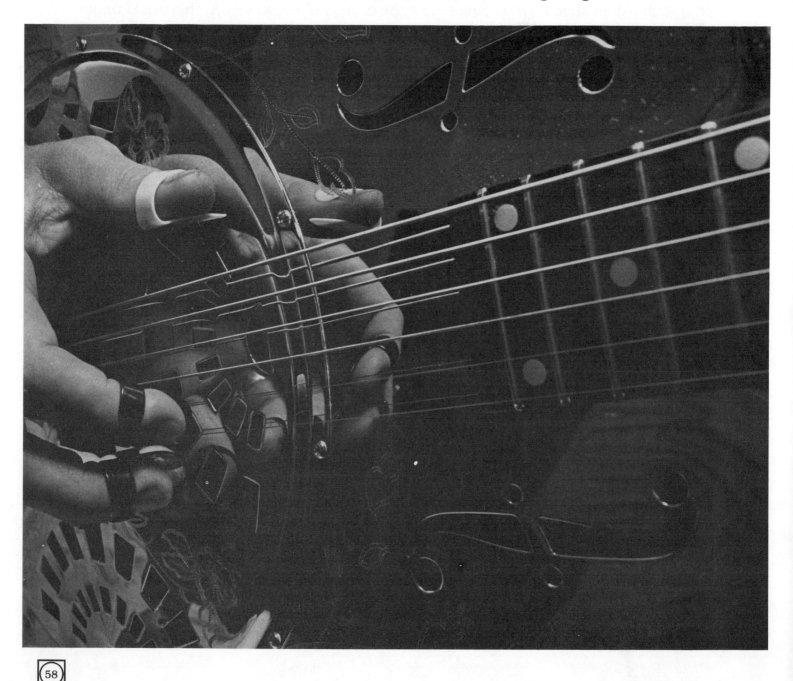

7. The Form

Funny thing about the blues. It has a very fixed structure compared to other kinds of music. That makes the mystery! Within its strict confines there is tremendous freedom. One of the greatest things about the blues is its simple form, that hides itself so many ways. The goal of the blues artist is to find new and different life in the form despite repetition of the pattern in song after song.

"Now when I say simple, I don't mean easy. I mean that the basic outline of the form is recognized by both musician and listener. The craft of filling in the form creates a common bond between all blues people that is not found among the more diversified, singular strands of popular music. This accounts for many chance meetings at studios where one blues musician would happen to run into another in the hallway and in the matter of a few minutes, make an historic first-cut record that stays with us forever.

"What I'm getting at — there isn't a tremendous middle ground for the artist. He is firmly held into the changes, and upon this he can literally count. But from this clockwork base, the pendulum swings the other way to delicate elaboration, off to the side remarks, simple statements with a held silence, crying out your feelings, one or two simple notes played over the bass note, or an understated vocal delivery that floats like a leaf on the way down. That's it, Boy. You will hear what I mean before I'm through with you.

"Now maybe you just thought I was passing the time of day when I told you to just snap your fingers in time. But I think that you know now, Boy. I think that you remember the four count. And the eight to the bar reference to the 'one and' sub-beat. Get off the train, Boy.

"Now count with me:

One, 2, 3, 4, Two, 2, 3, 4, Three, 2, 3, 4, Four, 2, 3, 4, Five, 2, 3, 4, Six, 2, 3, 4, Seven, 2, 3, 4, Eight, 2, 3, 4, Nine, 2, 3, 4, Ten, 2, 3, 4, Eleven, 2, 3, 4, Twelve, 2, 3, 4. Three sets of four count — that is the twelve bar blues. Now don't forget tempo, subdivision of the beat and accent are in on this, too. I won't say anything more about it right now. Just let it sink in for a minute.

"Yeah, the drums of Africa are still playing. That is why I showed you the beat first, Boy. The call and response was, as simple as it is, an evolution from the singing of one person. It is a fundamental way to repeat — I say it, you say it. The field people would count their work by it. We are stopping the spinning top to look at it, but when it is in motion it spins and spins and spins.

"Saying something twice is getting your point across. The double form eventually grew to three, that is the form AAA, and an American tradition was born. When Handy saw the guitarist from the boondocks that night at the turn of the century in Mississippi, he sang his verse three times. This was the traditional form that evolved into what we know as the twelve bar blues. That final third of the blues, the last count of four, is the part with the twist. At this point, the double statement is resolved, both poetically and musically.

"Let's not get in over our heads with a one-on-one account just yet. What I want you to see now is how we are going to assign tonal centers to be played over certain beats. You might get away with saying 'Play this chord when the beat gets to this point.' But there are more things to consider than what triad sounds right. You have the four string bass moving around the note. You can run your scales, play off the center with related chords. Yeah, just think in terms of one bass note for now and it would be best. Let's get you a guitar and check out the situation.

"The low E string played open is the first, or tonic in the key of E. The fourth of the scale is the open A string, and the fifth is the B note on the fifth string, second fret. Play quarter notes on these strings and just read across the top of the twelve bar beat diagrams as they are presented. Get ready.

"Here is a real early twelve bar form. Just make sure that you play the B note four times on the ninth count. Then A four more times and you stay down until the end. Go back to the first in your mind, but don't break the beat coming out of the twelfth bar. Just keep right on going.

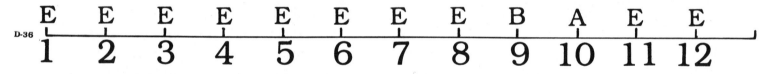

"This second one has the classic blues form which goes to the fourth at the fourth bar, then back to the tonic before it is resolved at the fifth at the ninth bar. The trail-off ending is still with us, so just stay in E until it begins again.

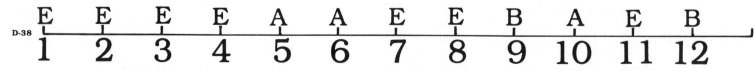

"The third one should have the spotlight, Boy, because it is the prime example. This is the true blue example. Please study it well. It starts at home for four straight bars, up to the fourth for two, then down again for two. Resolve at the ninth bar with the fifth, tenth bar is the step down, eleven is tonic again before the final resolution. You are going to resolve it twice in the last four bars. Do it now, Boy.

D-38

E	E	E	E	A	A	E	E	B	A	E	B
1	2	3	4	5	6	7	8	9	10	11	12

"The variations of this form go on and on, and as you listen to the music of the blues, you will be able to clearly recognize, after you know the game, what type of structure the performer is using. The next three examples are all the same except for the last bar. We have to go into subdividing the beat into four counts, that's quarter notes, in order to get the changes. Now you're the bass player, Boy. I thought you wanted to learn fast. Play the twelfth bar as it is prescribed — the first count of one gets an E note, the last three are picked up on B.

D-39
E	E	E	E	A	A	E	E	B	A	E	E B B B
1	2	3	4	5	6	7	8	9	10	11	12

"Now this guy divides the twelfth bar into half with the first two notes on E and the last two on B. I know it's not a big difference, it's only one note. But it can make a world of difference if you can't get it. It will bother you, and put you off. It won't let you in. You say to yourself 'skip it.' But the end of your fingertip says 'GET IT'.

D-40
E	E	E	E	A	A	E	E	B	A	E	E E B B
1	2	3	4	5	6	7	8	9	10	11	12

"Now this one uses the twelfth bar as a quick chromatic step triplet up to B. Keep it right on the beat. Don't try too hard — just get your strength and play it all the way through. Of the last four counts, only one is on B.

D-41
E	E	E	E	A	A	E	E	B	A	E	E A A# B
1	2	3	4	5	6	7	8	9	10	11	12

"You will hear this next one almost half the time on the old records. It is an old favorite because it breaks the sameness of the first four E bars by throwing in a bar of A count at the second bar. You will have fun going up to A here. You are only down on the tonic for a single bar, then your hand goes up to that other string. Understand that we can mix and match these critters like a bunch of little kids in the sandbox. You will understand the implications of tempo as soon as you roll the wheel enough times.

D-42
E	A	E	E	A	A	E	E	B	A	E	B
1	2	3	4	5	6	7	8	9	10	11	12

"This next twelve bar example subdivides the eleventh and twelfth bars by playing an alternate chord on the half-way mark. The thing here is, you have four chord centers to go to in the distance of two bars. If the tempo is running at a good clip, things really roll by in the blur of a single movement. At a slower tempo, you get a chance to subdivide the beat a little bit and you can ride the four chord change with a few lead notes on each change.

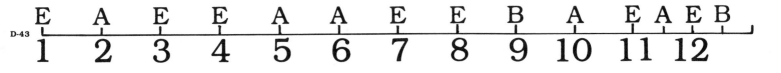

D-43
E	A	E	E	A	A	E	E	B	A	E A	E B
1	2	3	4	5	6	7	8	9	10	11	12

INTRODUCTIONS

"Introductions are common fare in all blues-based songs. The most common way is to start the introduction on the ninth bar of the common twelve bar structure. In other words, it's the last four bars. Remember, we are trying to look at this thing in lots of different ways, and one way to see it is in three, four bar segments. In this case, they start the song with the final group of four bars where the resolution takes place.

"Another common intro is the final two bars of the twelve bar. This is just enough time for the guitar to squeeze out a statement, or for a theme to run two bars before the fireworks start on square one. You can see that any of the varieties of twelve bar that have different changes in the final bars can also be used. Anything you can think of can be used. Wait until we get to playing some records. You're bound to hear anything start off a song. It's great.

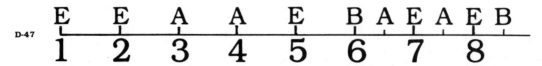

EIGHT BAR VARIETIES

"It's not over yet, because the blues also uses an eight bar structure to encompass its message. This form has a faster turnaround time, and the changes don't hang as long in one place. The relationship between the first and fourth and the fifth still stays the same, and so does the four/four time meter. The first bar bounces back around pretty fast, and this gives the form a feel of its own. Here is the first one I'll give you. Please notice that the sixth bar goes up to the fifth, just as the twelve bar structure did at the ninth bar.

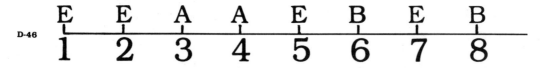

"This one stays the same as the first eight bar example for the first five bars, but subdivides the last three bars. We know a twelve bar example that got a similar treatment across the last two bars. Roll through all eight bars in a constant movement. Keep on the beat.

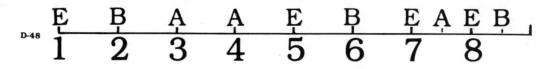

"This final example actually goes to B three different times. Right after the tonic first bar it goes to the fifth, a very effective move for grabbing attention. Notice that just the last two bars are subdivided.

D-48   E B A A E B E A E B
1 2 3 4 5 6 7 8

"For the sake of example, I have kept this presentation to the key of E. The one, four, five work themselves out in the key of A the same way as in the key of E. Witness the twelve bar in A.

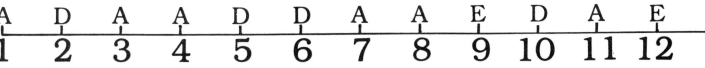

A	D	A	A	D	D	A	A	E	D	A	E
1	2	3	4	5	6	7	8	9	10	11	12

"Blind Lemon Jefferson used to throw in an extra bar to bring it to thirteen. But you see, this kind of thing results from getting the blues under your skin. You know it so well that you can fool with it. You can play what other types of musicians would call 'wrong notes' and just keep on going. After a while, some of the real deep delta stuff is sort of mesmerizing. You hear that tonic going on and on in a drone. The fourth adds that mirror to the first, but we are still waiting. Waiting for the fifth. And he might just hit off it once, but, Boy, get that timing and that is enough.

"If you play enough records, you're bound to hear what is known as an extended bridge. This takes the first four tonic bars of the twelve, and extends on four more identical tonic bars just to lengthen an interesting story that the driver is relating. After eight bars on the first, it goes straight into the normal fifth bar which is centered at the fourth.

"There are ways and there are ways, Boy. There are different ways to look at it. You can see it as a lot of lines, a lot of rules, a lot of information put in a list. I'm telling you, this is the blues — right here, right now. One problem with learning is that so much comes at you, that you sometimes forget — hey, the music."

The old man took the guitar from the boy's hands. "Let's just look at one form example. That way you can concentrate just in the example's singular sphere. We will give it this tempo and will subdivide it like this." The boy immediately sensed the transcedence of the old man once the strings started to play. It was music — one-note-at-a-time music. The twelve bars went by with such force that the boy's head was swimming.

The stark white light from the kitchen lamp made the list of forms on the table seem removed from the mood of the sound. "Now follow that form with your finger, Boy, and put the two together." Each bar rolled, each chord center came and went, each played its proud roll in the make-up of the whole cycle.

"I see it." The boy spoke plainly, removed from the music.

The old man stopped and grabbed his beer. "That, my boy, is how you teach guitar."

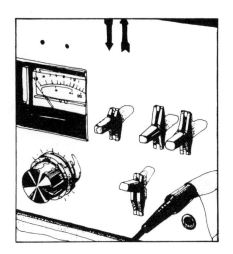

8. Blue Notes
The Five Note Blues

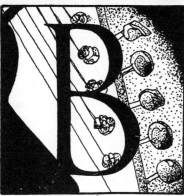

lue notes are two in number and originate from two altered major scale degrees which are commonly used in minor scale modes. We have established the major scale in all its glory between the space of one octave, and we know that it has an interval pattern of half and whole-steps. We also know that most music terminology is based upon the seven scale degrees of this diatonic scale. One through seven we have counted. Now I'm singing a new song. I'm telling you that the most important thing to the blues guitarist isn't the major scale, but of all things, A FIVE NOTE SCALE DERIVED FROM THE MAJOR. This is the blues scale. They don't call it the blues for nothing! This five note scale uses the two blue notes as its second and fifth degrees. What are these blue notes? How do they fit in with the major scale picture? How do they work to make this unique five note pentatonic blues scale? How, how, how?

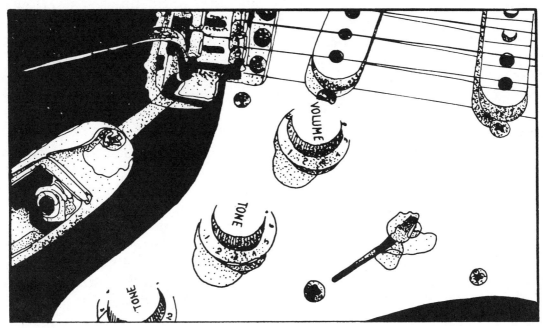

"Well, the guitar has a high E string and a low E string, right? So what I did is construct a fretboard diagram with the major scale on the low E string, with another fretboard showing us the blues scale, the new guy we're checking out, on the high E string. Here it is. Please note that degrees of both scales are given both numerically and alphabetically:

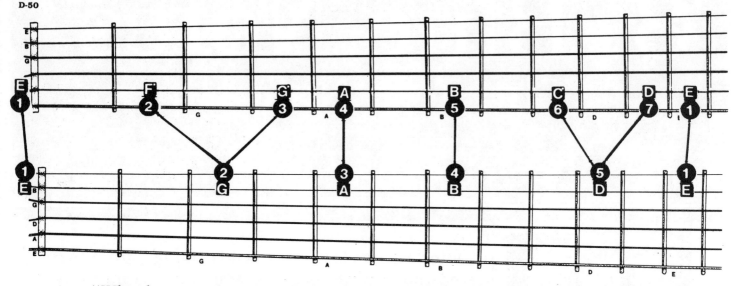

"What happened to our poor major scale to make it look like this, Boy? The term 'gapped scale' means a scale resulting from the omission of certain notes. The whole tone scale is the simplest example of a gapped scale because its interval pattern is six whole-steps in a row starting from the tonic. Just think about it, Boy, six scale degrees! Now I've really got you mixed up.

"Well, shake your head clear, Boy, or lose out. Here we go. The minor modes of the major are derived by lowering either the third, sixth or seventh scale degree by one half-step. Skip the numbers for a while and think about the effect of the minor notes on the listener. Try running your major scale, and after a few times through, jump out of the scale and pick the minor third just once. This is the note three frets up from the tonic. Just let it resound. The flatted seventh will do the same thing — I can't describe it verbally. It is a sure guess that it has something to do with the ratio of the frequency to the tonic and the way that the brain interprets the sound. Now that is a sad note. The word melancholy comes to mind because these off-notes envoke some kind of low tension.

"The flatted third and flatted seventh are the blue notes, and as you have seen from the last diagram, they take two of the five notes in the blues scale. How did the blues scale get to be five notes? Well, when the major scale is altered to make the minor scale, the position of the degrees changes a little but the number of degrees remains at seven. The blues scale eliminates the second and the sixth to bring the number of scale degrees down from seven to five. In other words, the second and the third come together at the midway point, the chromatic step between them, and stay there. It's the same deal for the sixth and seventh degree. This results in a five-note scale that has two intervals that are a distance of three frets. The interval pattern of the blues scale in chromatic steps reads: 3, 2, 2, 3, 2. The basic centers that we use for the building of triads to make blues chords, THE FIRST, THE FOURTH AND THE FIFTH, are common to both the blues and major scale. Now go back and look at the diagram of the two scales, again, Boy.

"Up to this point I have always tried to maintain an overview scope of things, witness The Range We Live. I keep reminding you of the twelve fret repeating pattern for any and all scales. You know, things like that. Let's pull down our sails and set another course for awhile. Those waters are expansive and dynamic, but also rough, as your range of dimension is so often shocked. Let's pull into a quiet, still-water lagoon. We'll go to smaller places where we can really get a look at one example and get the most out of it. I know that it's a lot of material to be presented with a whole new scale just after you were starting to get familiar with the major. But this is the one that you will use. I want to show you this new scale all over the board in both the keys of E and A. Then I want to show you how to use it. I want to show you little things about it. You learn in little bits even at best, Boy. So we must settle in.

"First off, let's run the chromatic scale in E starting on the low E string open. Play each note chromatically, one finger per fret, using the open strings, until you get to the octave E note on the fourth string second fret.

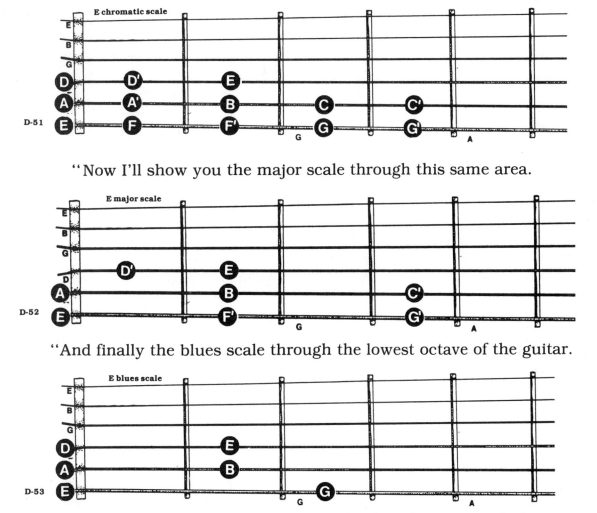

"Now I'll show you the major scale through this same area.

"And finally the blues scale through the lowest octave of the guitar.

"Now that you know the blues scale on the three low strings, let's move it on up into the next higher octave that ends on the E note of the open first string. I put one more note on top of the octave — the flatted third — so that you can see the emerging pattern.

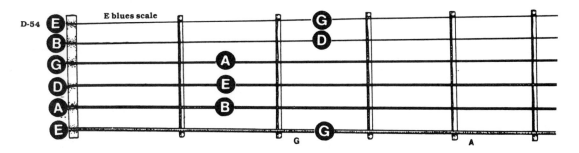

"Welcome home. You have arrived, Boy. I finally have a chance to show you the most basic position for blues lead guitar. This one position is very special because it has notes from the blues scale across all six strings. This line of notes appears only one place in the twelve fret repeating pattern, and that is the fret where the tonic note is played on the E string. You see, in the case of E, the open strings represent the 'zero' fret. I'll go over that more in a minute. Right now, just stare at this baby. You have all the strings open so you can work right over top of them. That's three frets up for the first, second and sixth string, and two frets up for the third, fourth and fifth string. Since this spot is so important, let me give you another diagram that sheds a little more light on this position.

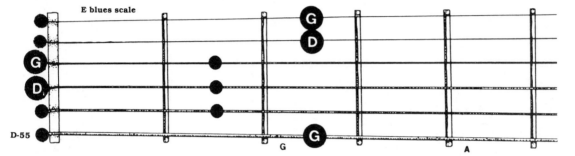

"This diagram shows you which of the scale degrees are the minor blue notes. One way to pick them out — when you see the large interval of three frets, the upper note is Blue."

ONE HUNDRED TIMES

The old man stood up from the kitchen table quickly and asked the boy to follow. "Sometimes it is necessary to change in order to bring about a new mood. Right now I want to just leave our papers on the table as they are and go up on the roof and put down some sounds. Come on." They went up through three flights of old wooden stairway until a hatch in the attic roof gave access to a small platform on the rooftop that was surrounded by railing. "Now I know that this is going to sound crazy, Boy, but I want you to play that basic box I just showed you."

"Doesn't sound crazy to me, Old Man," the boy said as he fingered the box up and down.

"Well, what's crazy, Boy, is that I want you to descend and then ascend through the scale ONE HUNDRED TIMES."

"I see what you mean about crazy now, Old Man."

"Well, you asked me to teach you the blues, and this is my way. It depends on what you want to do. You can study just the dry paperwork if you are so inclined. But if you ever want to get up on stage and play at that party, it's one hundred times! This is the beginning of the movie, Jack. It doesn't mean a thing. Tomorrow you will know it. I'm willing to sit here like a fool and count out every time through for you. What more can I do, Boy? I thought you said you wanted to make it."

The boy drew in a sharp breath and started to climb down, and then up through the scale.

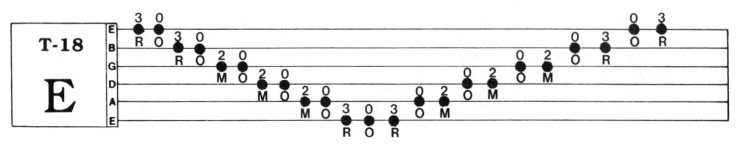

"One, very good Boy. Two, that's it. Three ... Four ... Five ... Six ... Keep it up." This went on and on through the numbers up to fifty. "Fifty-one, you've got it Boy. Fifty-two, yes, yes, yes. Fifty-three." Never once did the old man let up until ten minutes later. "Ninety-eight. Ninety-nine. ONE HUNDRED!!! That's it, Boy. Tomorrow you will know!" Immediately the old man led the boy back to their homework papers on the kitchen table.

E BLUES BOARD

"You know that each scale has a twelve fret territory and you know that portion of the five note blues scale that takes up three or four frets down at the bottom in E. I will now present you with the entire repeating pattern for the blues scale in the key of E between the open strings and the twelfth fret, where you will find the same line-up that you get on the open strings.

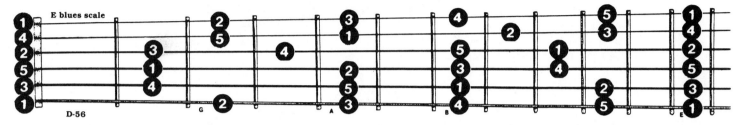

"Do you see the part of this pattern that you played on the roof? Can you see the scale degrees on the low E and high E strings are the same? Do you see the pattern on the fifth string carries the same code that the sixth string has from the fifth fret up? You know that all six open strings can be played open, so look across the fifth and fourth frets for the notes of the open strings. Can you see the tonic notes as they appear? Let me cut down some trees here so you can see the first of the scale.

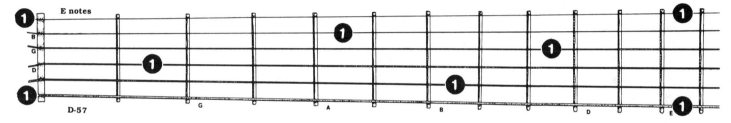

"Here is an interesting formula that you can see applied in this diagram. There are four easy ways to find the same note on the board in another place. You can always go up twelve frets, if you have the room. If the original note appears on either the sixth or fifth string, you can go over two thinner strings, and then up two frets and you have your octave. If the original note is on the third or fourth string, you can go over two thinner strings and then up three frets. The final way is if you have a note in the middle of the board, you can go over one thinner string and down five frets. The exception here is the four-fret difference for the note found on the third string — that annoying half-step odd ball presented by the second string. You know, all guitarists live with that irregularity.

THE ROOT NOTE FRET

"Only one fret of the twelve in the total blues pattern has notes across all six strings. That is the twelfth fret for the key of E. The open strings can be counted as a 'zero' root note fret for E. The root note fret occurs only where the tonic note is centered on the low and high E string. Knowing this fret and understanding how it is moved is essential to your guitar playing. Look closely at this diagram which shows you how the root note fret came about in E and how the same arrangement looks in the keys of G and A.

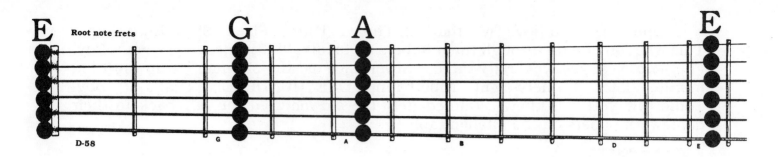

"So here is something to remember. If you want to play in G, you move this unique position up to the third fret and play across this fret using the index to finger the strings on the third fret, and the ring, middle or pinky to play the notes from the scale that falls above. Look across the fifth fret and you will see the notes that make up the blues scale in the key of A. You will get to know the deal with the root note fret by using it. Just remember, once you locate one root note fret, there is another twelve frets higher.

BLUES SCALE FINGERINGS IN E

"The time has come to take you through the blues scale in all of the positions so you will know the pattern in its entirety. You already know it at the basic position, but there are several intermediate positions that you should know between the two root note frets. We will start at the bottom in E blues and work ourselves up just like we did with the major scale. Each position gets its own transcription. Limber up, Boy. Here we go with the first of seven for E blues. I know that it is the same one from the roof, but just play it, Boy. It is still your friend!

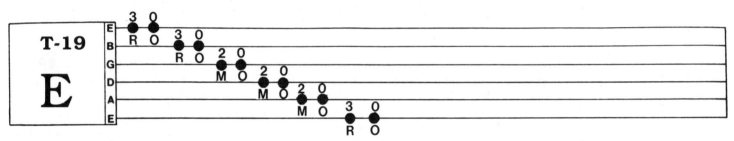

"Here is the same position with a different way to finger it. The diagram is the same as for the last one.

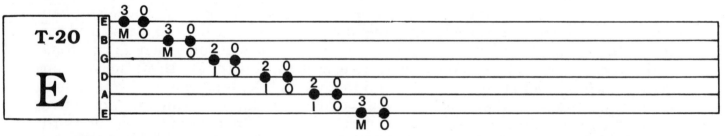

"We are now going to wander out of our known territory into the area just above the basic first position. Once you know the bottom position, you can confidently jump up to these notes and play them. They are all in the scale, why not?

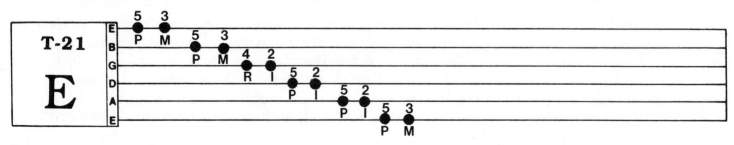

"The fourth way through takes us right into the middle ground between the open strings and the twelfth fret. This position is used a lot. There are two positions above and there are two positions below, so you are going to get those middle steps — the fourth and the fifth of the major — on both your E strings. It's pretty much a whole step sequence except for the second and third string, so look for the blue notes to stand on the upper note at these intervals.

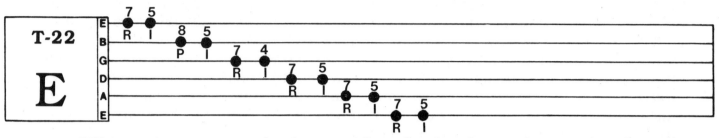

"This next guy goes up the distance of another hand toward our goal at the root note twelfth fret. The next one will arrive at the root note from the bottom. This one works pretty much across the seventh fret except for the second string. It is pretty close to our basic number one position with two exceptions which you can immediately spot.

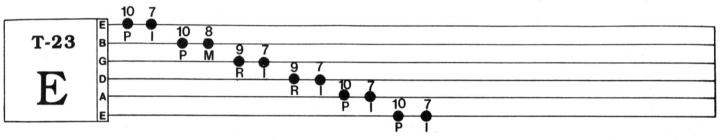

"Check out the root note fret here. We are looking at it from the basement, whereas up on the roof you were running on top of it. You have a well-proportioned pattern here, so knock it out. Pinky plays every note on twelve.

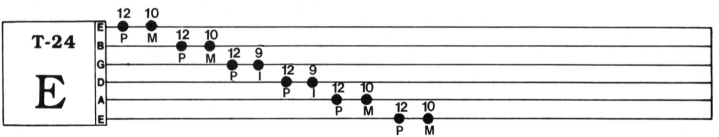

"Yeah, we have run it up. Here we are in the basic position for the blues scale but this time we are at the twelfth fret. We have covered the whole pattern and then some. Go ahead and do it just for fun, Boy. I know you already know it. Make sure to use the pinky on this example just for the sake of seeing how it works. When you actually play at this position for E, you might want to use the ring for those notes on the fifteenth fret.

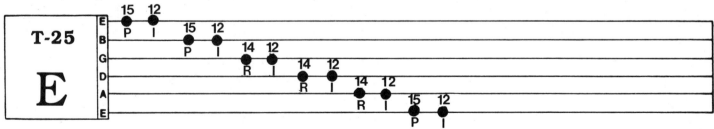

"One of the nice things about having the root note fret exposed above and below is that it allows access to both sides. You can run riffs right through it if you combine the boxes. There is no law against it.

BLUES SCALE FINGERINGS IN A

"What is unique about the blues scale in the key of A? Well it starts with a tonic note played on the fifth string open rather than the sixth string you use for E. You will now have to change your thinking around to all of the various A notes that are on the board. The blues scale degrees for the key of A are the same as the dots you see up the fifth string: A, C, D, E and G. These are the same as the notes across the fifth fret. The big thing that you have to know about blues in A is that the root note fret works out on the fifth fret. We aren't going to go up on the roof this time, but go ahead and play this basic A position fifty times anyway." The boy knew better than to object, so he set his fingers to the board.

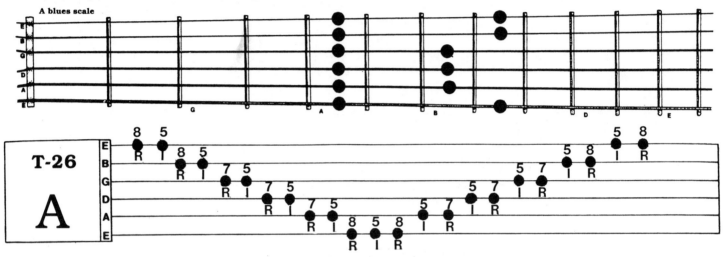

Just like before, the old man patiently counted out the cycles through the A blues scale. After fifty times the old man was laughing.

"You're giving me the blues, alright, Old Man. Now I have blue fingers!"

"Don't worry about it, Boy. Who remembers practice hours when the amps are roaring and people are running around?

"I can't tell you how important this basic position is to your playing. We might touch down on a subject like equal temperament for a few minutes just because it is history. But, Boy, what you just played is the game. The notes on and around the root note fret. Let's jump into the fire again and get through these six fingerings for the blues scale in A. Then we will tie up a few loose ends and move on to technique. The first thing that we have to do is study the A blues scale pattern as it covers the board.

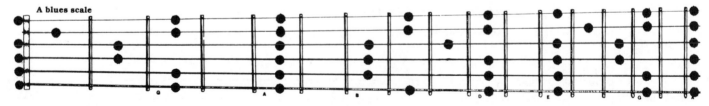

"Let's stare at it, Boy. Here's a cup of tea. Wake up. Talk to me, Boy."

"Well, Old Man, I see the root note fret at the fifth fret and I see it again at the seventeenth. I see the pattern that worked below the root note twelfth fret is now down underneath the fifth. I see the tonic centers on the E strings at the fifth fret and on the open A string."

The old man placed another diagram on the table. "Here are the rest of the A centers, Boy.

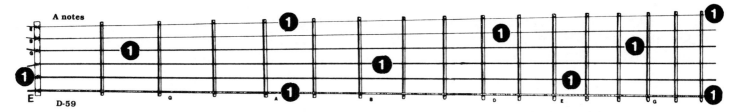

"If you're ready to subdivide the pattern, then don't stop me, Boy. The first way we have already been over. But just like we did in E, we will go over all of them once and have them together one after another for your study reference. Here is the first one:

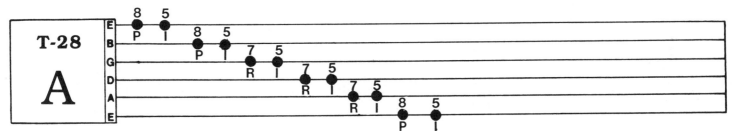

"Here is another fingering for the same pattern. Instead of using just the ring finger for every note above the root note, use the pinky for the three fret intervals. Do it again.

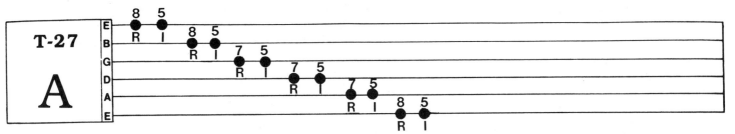

"Rather than go up, we are going to travel below the root note fret on this next one. This is the same position that we had to wait until the end to show in the key of E because of the situation with the open strings for that key. Don't forget. I won't hold you to these fingerings when we start to make music, but I want you to go through them the way they are transcribed for now. That means using the pinky across the fifth fret for this one.

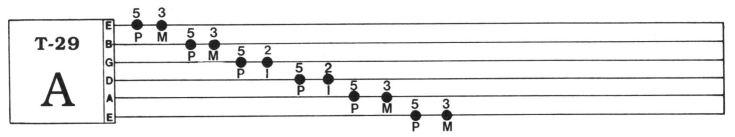

"The next one will show you the position for the A blues scale using the open strings. They are all played open with the exception of that one odd ball at the first fret of the second string. Check out the blue notes played above the low two strings at the third fret. You will use parts of this pattern extensively, building the blues scale on and around the major A chord played at the bottom.

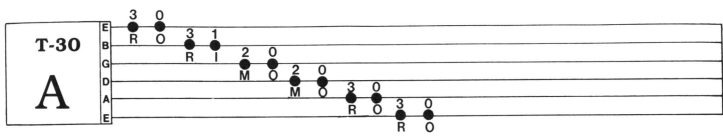

"Now we are moving into the area just above the basic pattern played above the root note fret. Maybe it has occured to you by now that the patterns for the key of A are the same as for the key of E with the number five added to each of the transcription numbers. It's no big deal — it's just the way it is.

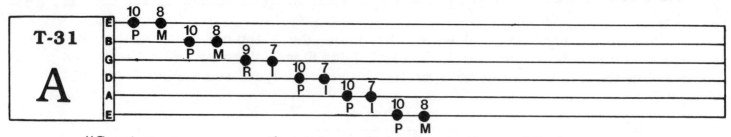

"Coming up, we cover that intermediate area in the middle between the two root note frets. In the case of the key of A, that means centering between the fifth and seventeenth fret. You should remember this one from E. It's the same except for its position.

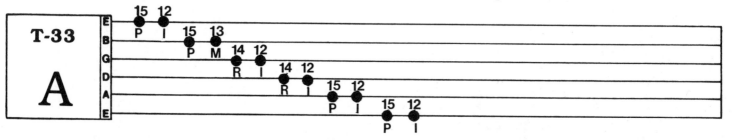

"This last one is the same pattern that you play when you are centered at the open strings. That's the reason for all of the twelfth fret notes you have to play with the index finger. Watch for the oddball on the second string.

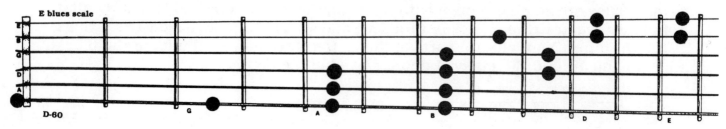

"Now before we give it up, I want to talk to you just for a second. The whole pattern is important. That is why we studied it piece by piece. These fingerings stand on their own as fingering exercises. But what I think you really want to know is how and where the scale is primarily used and drill yourself at that point. This area is on and around the root note fret. One other thing — these boxes are arbitrary divisions. You can run right through them from the top, out the bottom if you can think to do it. Now here is an example of what I'm talking about in the key of E. This is bound to wake you up!

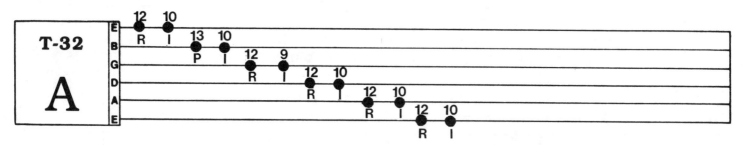

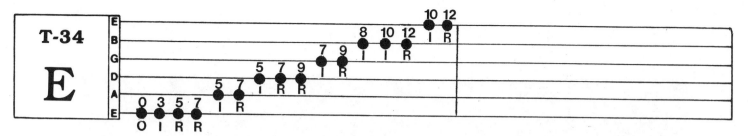

"Just went through a few boxes and didn't even stop to think about it. That is what it is all about, Boy. You teach yourself guitar, really. Now with this next passage I will center you into the fifth fret of the A blues scale. Watch what happens when we combine notes from below and above the root note fret into the same passage."

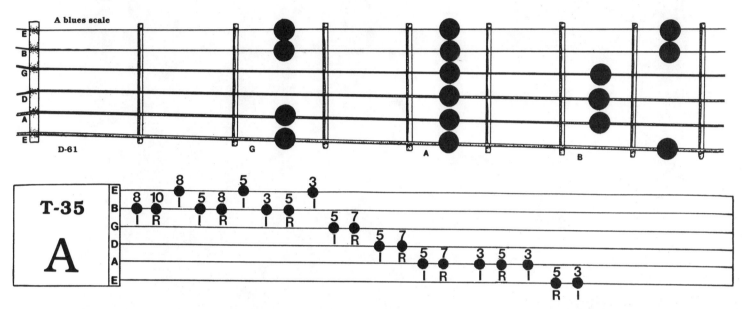

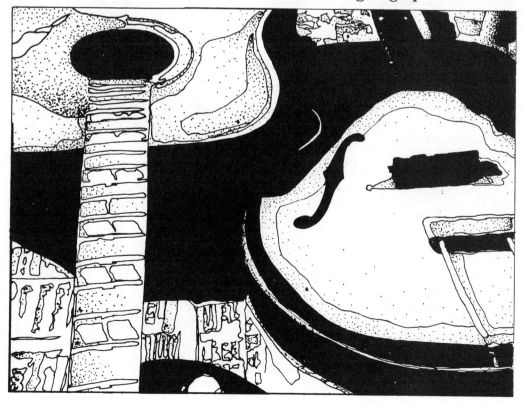

The old man set into the boy again. "Now I want to show you how. . ."

But that was all he could get out. Walking for the door, the boy grabbed his guitar and said, "See you in an hour, Old Man. I'm going up on the roof!"

9. Techniques, Tactics and Procedure

K eep your wits about you,'' the old man proclaimed as he climbed out of the hatch and onto the roof. "We are destined to jump out of our frying pan and into the fire itself.'' The boy had been practicing his blues scale fingerings for one hour and was ready for the old man's intensity.

"What is the fire, Old Man? I think I know about the frying pan.''

"The fire is the underly ing force that powers expression. This quality cannot be indicated by notes, signs or symbols of any kind. You have to be aware of your own touch, Boy. This goes for everything across the board: the dynamics of the note, the nuances of tempo, phrasing, accenting and all the techniques that affect the texture of the note.

"There is no doubt about one thing — you have to know your scales first. The finer points will come after you have conquered the patterns. You must have the blues.pattern down cold for this reason: it will soon be used as an underlying pattern over which another will be placed. If you don't know the first one, forget it. I'm glad to see you practice, Boy. As I look at you now, I know that between your ears someplace you have those notes stored away. The more you play them, the more you can draw on them with familiar confidence. Hear what I'm saying now, Boy. Know your blues scale in E and A. We will surely cover each of the finer techniques as soon as I am sure you know enough about the blues scale. This thing has a familiar pattern. You see, it looks like this across any one given key centered fret.

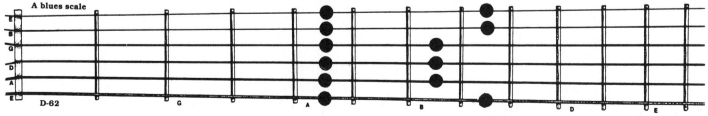

"You see the fun thing about it is that if you just let yourself go, you can see it in all kinds of ways. Now given, it's not as complex a subject as, say, nuclear physics or let's say, the history of the railroad in California. But, man, I do know how to play it.''

The boy stood up and reached out to the air. "Then teach me the blues scale and how to use it. Hurry, Old Man. Teach me everything now, before morning!" The old man nodded. "You are alright, kid. I'll teach you everything I can in a short time. Here, check this out if you think you know the blues scale.

"At the bottom we can look at it any number of different ways. Here are three examples off the top of my head, Boy. The first one, the blues according to the major scale degrees; the second one, you see the tonic; the third, the major triad comes out. How're you doing, Boy?"

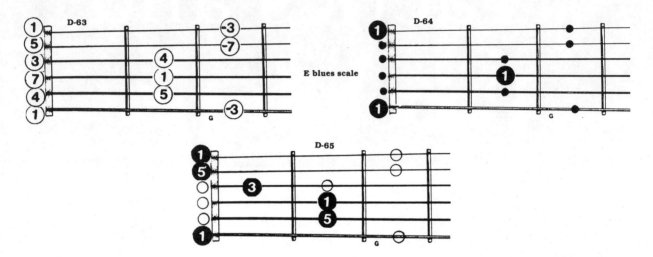

"Keep on painting the picture, Old Man." "Okay, if that's what you want, Boy. Let me see you do this. Straight key of E. Blues.

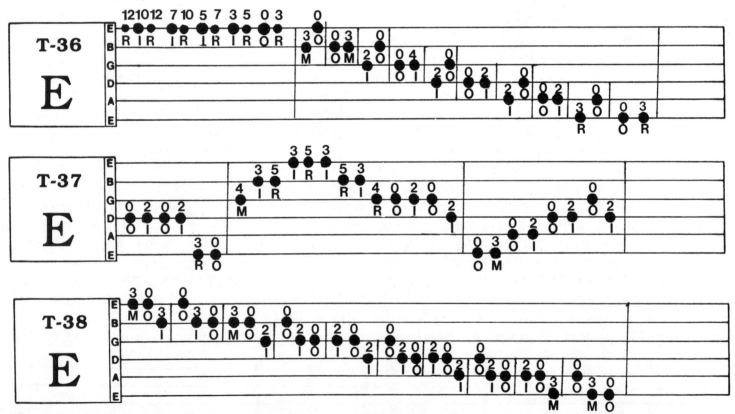

"Now, let's look at a basic triplet in both keys. There are five notes in the scale, right? Well, if you add an additional lower tonic note, you have six. Walk this guy down: one, two, three; one two, three. Count these six notes every octave. We are dealing with two octaves across the field, so look for two sets of two triplets. That's four altogether straight across the open strings in the key of E at the bottom. The same triplets are also shown in the key of A at the fifth fret. One last thing before I play — the last note of the second triplet and the first note of the third triplet are the same tonic note. Just play it twice and go.

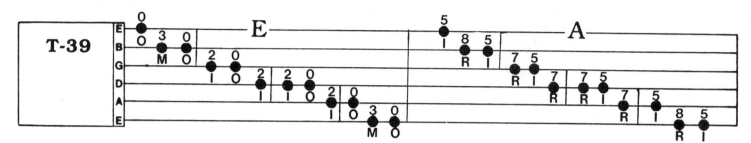

"You're lucky to be here tonight, Boy, because I'm beginning to give away some pretty heavy secrets. Now, watch the dot size closely. Don't just pass over it. Play one note twice as long as the other. Watch the triplets change.

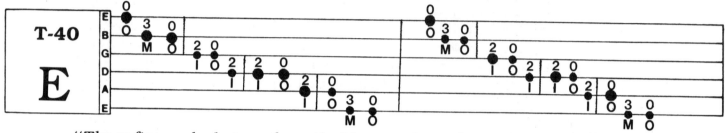

"Those five scale degrees from the blues scale work together to make up a long chain of notes that we play across the octaves on ascending strings. In time, you will see the whole woods. But, Boy, it doesn't ever get to the point where you will know each song on the radio before it happens. Nay, not each incarnation. But study the elements, the signposts of each dimension. Then nothing will blow your head off. If it does, tune in and figure it out, wow, you can learn anything. Even the greatest have five fingers and a guitar that won't tune. Believe me.

"Let's get down to basics, Boy. You play, I say. You ready?" The boy was leaning against the railing with his hands on the guitar. His voice matched the old man. "You call it. I'm waiting." "Okay, I'll give you three warm up runs. Now don't say to yourself 'I know that.' That is like a runner saying, 'Oh, I know that track field.' Hey Boy, how about running? Ten times each.

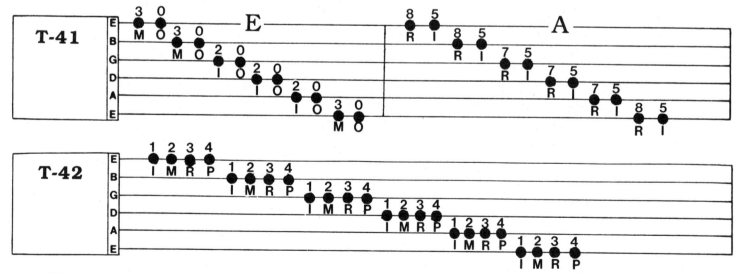

FOUR FINGER WALKS

"Now direct your attention to the final grouping. This is a chromatic fingering exercise that uses the numbers one through four to name the fret which is played. The fingering stays consistent throughout. Now I drew up these exercises for you to go through based on the numbering sequence of the last example. Keep in the same position down at the bottom, but go with the sets of numbers. Use the four number code to work out the sequence for each set. Then work the sequence across all six strings.

$$1\ 2\ 3\ 4, \quad 1\ 2\ 4\ 1, \quad 1\ 3\ 1\ 4, \quad 1\ 3\ 4\ 2,$$

$$4\ 3\ 2\ 1, \quad 1\ 2\ 4\ 2, \quad 1\ 3\ 2\ 4, \quad 1\ 3\ 4\ 3.$$

$$1\ 2\ 1\ 4, \quad 1\ 2\ 4\ 3, \quad 1\ 3\ 4\ 1,$$

SWING THE PICK

"Got blues scale in A at the fifth fret. By now, you can just wind up the left hand and let it play. So why don't you? We are looking at the pick hand now. See the transcription.

"The up-and-down picking symbols are waiting for you, Boy. Hold the pick tightly and bear down. Just shine the light of your eyes on the scene and you will have done enough. Look at how you rest your hand. Now run this exercise up and down a few times and you will immediately establish your own limit. After a few times through, speed up the tempo and just top the note. Get it to sound like a chirp. Just touch down on the notes like a stick against a picket fence.

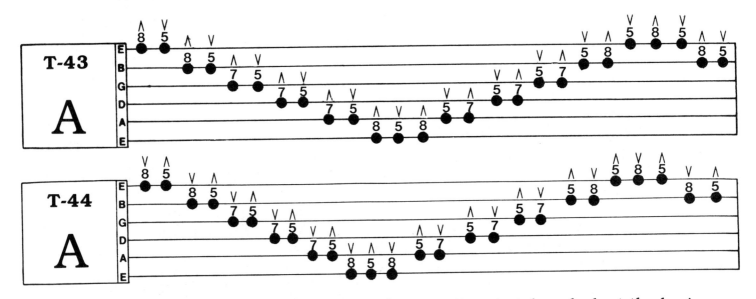

"Moving on to other things, I think that it is time to take a look at the basic techniques one at a time. There are five of these techniques: bending, pulling, hammering, sliding and vibrato. Right now, I want to show you something about the index finger. Music is a very universal science, but like other things, we eventually have to adapt it to the human scale. This is the reason there are all of these scale patterns. If we had ten fingers, those patterns would look a little bit different. In turn, each musical instrument has a range of notes that it plays called its *compass*, and certain peculiar characteristics are unique to each instrument. Blues guitarists brought out all of the extremes of the guitar. Turning their backs on tradition, they wanted the thing to sound bad, slightly out of tune, a mirror of their crying voice. They broke all of the rules, but more than anything else, *they gravitated to the easiest position for the left hand.* Before we jump into technique, I want to show you one of these easy positions. Just place the last joint of the index finger across the two thinnest strings at the fifth fret. Everything sort of comes together at this one point.

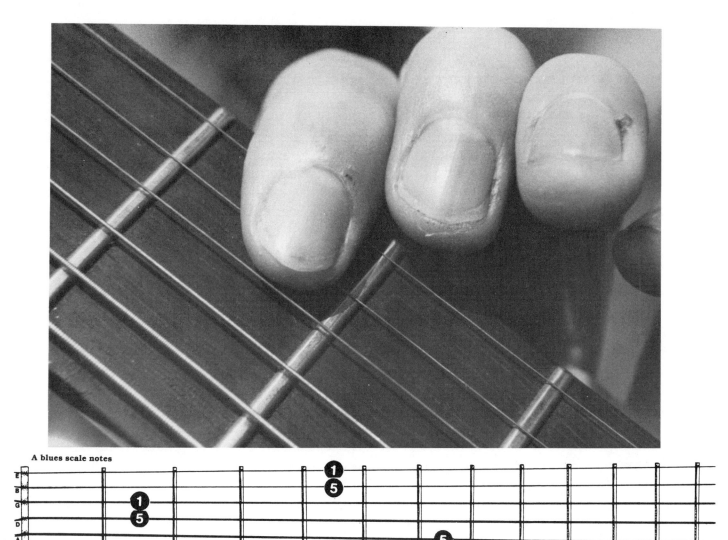

A blues scale notes

"This diagram shows you the spot we are talking about on the thin strings along with two other positions in A. These two notes are the first and the fifth of the scale — *two notes from the basic triad.* The lead guitarist places his index across this position using the index as a mini-bar. In the key of E, the two open thin strings do the job, but you have no control over those notes other than to let them sound. The index can be moved to accommodate any root note fret, and is an easy way to center your leadwork. Here is the heart of the basic box. Notes from the blues scale are ready to be played immediately above and below the index in this double string position with the other fingers. You can even move the double deal two frets below, or three above, and still grab only blues scale degrees. Lead guitarists know this sort of stuff from sheer exploration and discovery. It's easy to do.

BENDING

"We know that the guitar has strings that stretch over frets and when we put the flesh of our finger down on that string, we bring it to a shorter length — thus, it vibrates at a higher frequency. Now, if you take your finger and push it across the fret, you are fooling around with a determined formula [Appendix 5]. The string length stays basically the same, but you change the tension and this raises the pitch of the note. Any string can be bent by any finger at any fret. You can pluck, bend and relax, or you can bend, pluck then relax. You can bend toward the thick strings, the thin strings, or swing across the mid-point on your way to doing both. There is also a factor of how far to bend any given note.

"Our first bent string example uses the ring finger to bend the note found on the third string/eighth fret. Before you do anything, plant the index across the two thin strings at the fifth fret. Pluck and bend your ring finger note and push it until it sounds the note normally played on the ninth fret of the third string. This is a half-step bend which sounds the same note that is held by the index finger on the second string. Now try bending your note, and immediately afterwards, play the double notes held by the index. This is basic bent note stuff for the blues and rock guitarist. What it boils down to is starting out on a chromatic degree below the fifth of the major on the third string/eighth fret, bending the note up to sound the fifth, and then sounding those guys held with the index. Here is the lowdown on the riff.

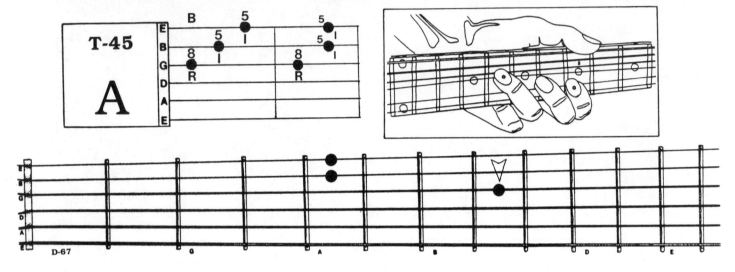

"Keep your index finger where it is and try bending the eighth fret of the second string with your ring finger. Pluck it and bend it hard to sound the A note normally sounded on the tenth fret. This is the same tonic note held by the index on the first string. This is a harder bend than the first example because it pushes up the pitch of the note a whole-step.

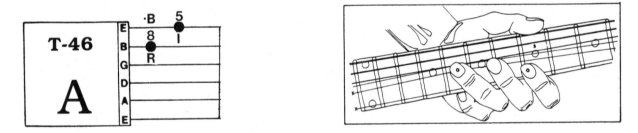

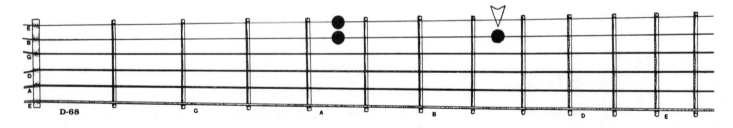

"The two examples that we have looked at are basic, but many more bent string positions are considered common. This is the kind of thing you can figure out on your own just by giving it a little time. Here are a few more examples of how we can bend a note and then go to an adjacent string to grab another note. All are shown in the key of A.

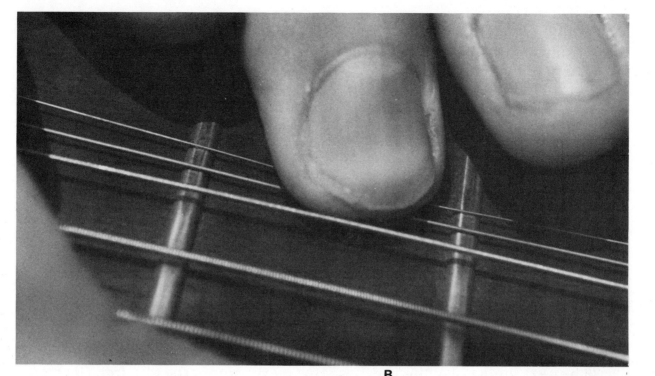

"You can bend more than one string at a time and there is no law that says you have to bend a note at least one half step. You can pluck a note and just move it slightly across the board giving texture to the note. This is how guitarists get their axe to talk.

PULLING

"Okay, let's keep the index planted across those thin strings at the fifth fret. Now fret the note played by the ring finger on the first string/eighth fret. Pluck the string as usual, and then snap your finger off the string in the direction away from the other strings in such a way that the string is set vibrating. This sounds the note held by the index without actually having to pick it. Here's the diagram:

A blues scale notes

D-69

"Pulling in the key of E is cool because you can sound that open string just by pulling off above it, even with the index. As a matter of fact, here is one to try on for size. It is a pull-off note, that pulls off onto another pull-off note. Got that? Just study the info for a minute and you will get it. Ring and index only. Pick only the first note of every three notes.

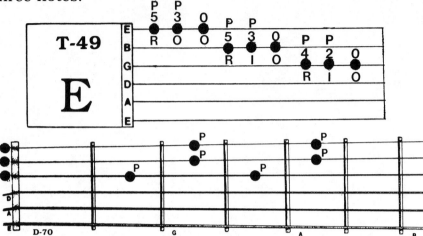

"The next thing is a pulling exercise that works across the fifth fret. Get ready to plant the index across all five, moving as you go. Use the pinky to pull off the notes freted three frets above the root note fret. The ring is going to pull off the rest of the two fret intervals. Work yourself back and forth across the fret pulling every other note.

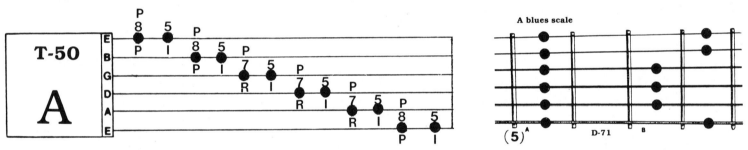

"Pulling can increase your speed of playing, and has a distinct sound of its own because the string is slightly bent before the finger comes all the way off. The technique is very effective on electric, but if you listen to the early blues records, you can hear those guys pulling notes on an acoustic, down at the bottom in E.

HAMMERING

"Hammering is coming down strong with a fretting finger onto the string in order to sound a note. You can pluck an open string and hammer it down to the second fret. The string was vibrating when it was hammered, so the new note sounds from the hammering and the momentum of the vibration from the earlier pluck.

"This technique is usually carried out by the ring or middle finger, over the top of a note held by the index finger. Try hammering on each note of the blues scale degrees above the open strings in the key of E.

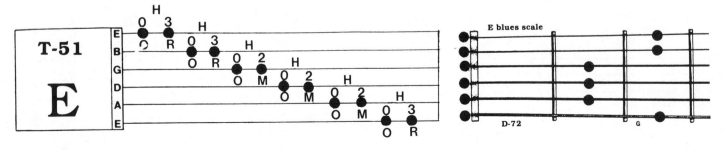

"We're getting there. Just one more set of exercises with the hammer. First, a word on the repeated hammer. You bring the finger down on the string and it is a hammer. You pull it off and it's a pull-off. Both techniques involve setting the string in motion and keeping it going. Try hammering the note on, then pulling it off, then hammering on immediately again and again. This results in a quick flurry of two distinct notes with no picking necessary. This is great blues stuff for lead guitar, especially over the open strings in the key of E or A. Try a repeat hammer on the tonic E at the fourth string/second fret over the open string. All of those hammer positions work great above those open strings. Here are the final hammer-on exercises that I promised. The repeat hammer is to be employed on the third set after the bar line.

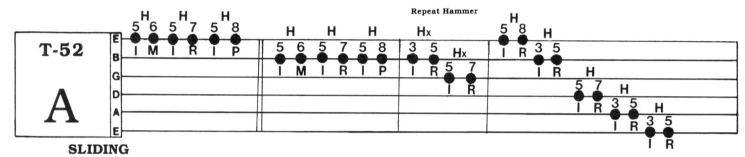

SLIDING

"Sliding sort of speaks for itself. You can sound a note and then take it up and over a fret, or down over a fret. You can slide over one fret, or all the way down or up. That string will keep vibrating so you can hear it producing a note all the way up or down. There isn't a lot to say about the slide, except its use is what will make your style more versatile. Here are exercises to tune you into some of the possibilities. The first one is a way of playing the same note twice. The second one shows you a movable chord situation that you can slide as a unit which moves several ringing strings over a fret at the same time.

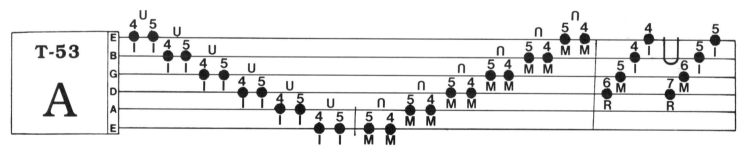

VIBRATO

"When you play a note on a piano, you hit a key which moves a hammer that hits the fixed string. You have little control over the tonal quality of the note. The guitar's fret system makes us texture the tone of every note we fret — whether we want to or not. Any movement on the string changes the note slightly. The game with vibrato is to consciously roll the finger in the direction of the string's length between two frets. This exposes the finger to a greater length of string than normal, and produces a turning sort of sound like the original revolving horn Leslie cabinet used with organs. Vibrato is a little more subtle and controllable than the bend technique and can be applied with a quick repeating movement that makes a tremolo sound called the trill. This hand movement shakes like you are using an eraser on a pencil. B. B. King plays tight vibrato to sing each note of his sparse style. Run with me a while, Boy. We will put together a few passages using combinations of technique.

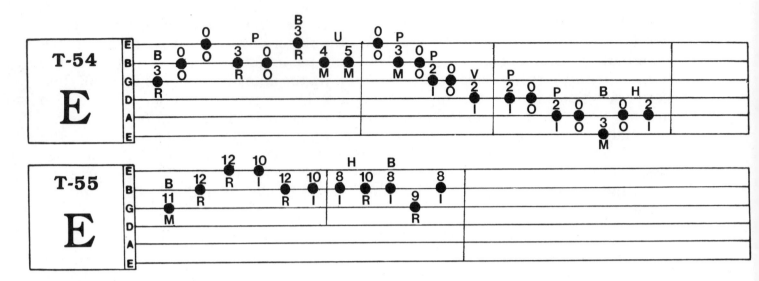

DOUBLE Es, DOUBLE Bs

"Here is a riff that takes advantage of the open thin strings. To get our double E notes, take the ring finger and place it on the second string/third fret. Now, pluck it and slide it up to the fifth fret, playing the open E string at the same time. Now move it down and play the third string/third fret with the middle and slide it up to the fourth fret, playing the note on the open B string at the same time. These examples both end with the same note but at different positions. It is good to know them in this position because you become visually oriented to the open E and B strings, and to their sound-alike brother notes on the adjacent strings.

"One more slide that I'll throw in for good measure is the index across the two thin strings, just like we placed them before. But this time sound them on the fret below where you want to go, and slide them over the fret together.

"Here's the low down.

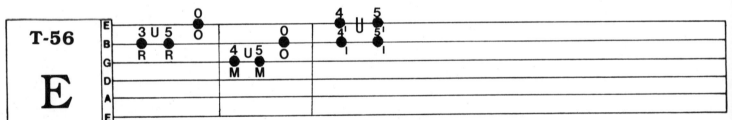

E AND A WINDOWS

"One of the greatest things about the blues pattern is its versatility. If you really want to know both the keys of E and A, it is often helpful to compare riffs from one key to the other. That is what we are going to do here. The riffs might not be exactly the same, but study them closely because everything has its reason.

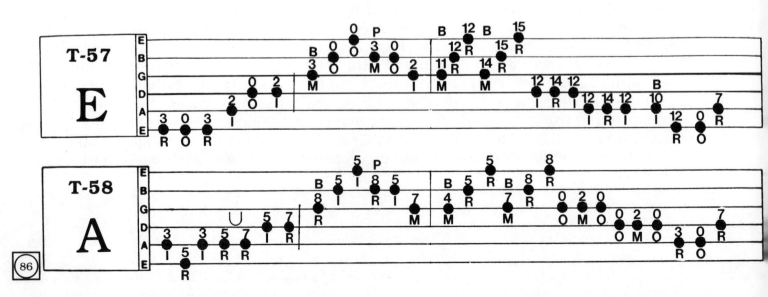

CENTERING

"We have talked about the first, the fourth and the fifth enough. Now it's time for you to get familiar with where they are centered. First off, we will make up a small chart to tune us into the structure.

$$
\begin{array}{cccc}
 & \text{1st} & \text{4th} & \text{5th} \\
\text{E} - & \text{E} & \text{A} & \text{B} \\
\text{A} - & \text{A} & \text{D} & \text{E}
\end{array}
$$

"Out of six possible positions, we have to worry about recognizing only four because two, the E and A, are common to both keys. E is the first of E and the fifth of A. A is the first of A and the second of E.

"Now, the way I want to do this is to 'build' a fifth above each of the first, the fourth, and the fifth of the keys E and A. This is not a chord, but a *tone cluster* comprised of two notes. All that you have to know is that it's two notes from the chord in a regular configuration. Here is how it was derived out of our two favorite chords.

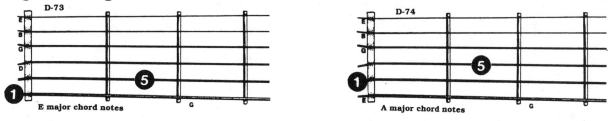

"I'm going to give you a five position series for E and five more for A. These are not arrangements. Each series is three places where you will find the first, the fourth and the fifth positions so you can put the fifth above each degree. You have to go back to your form papers, play these guys instead of the open strings that I had you play at the time. Here is the transcription:

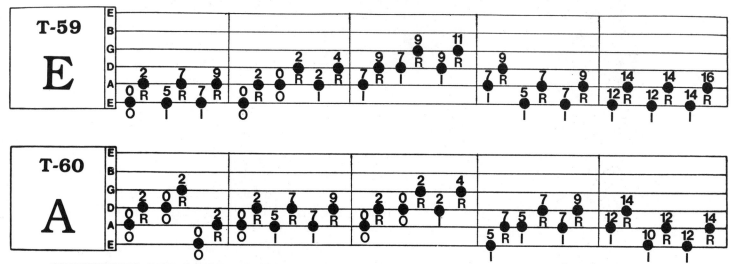

STRUMMING THE CHORD WITH TIME

"How do those rhythm guitarists do it? It's a broad enough field that they have their own hat-full of tricks. The prospect of combining two complex vehicles such as chords and rhythms is one that you will have to study in depth if you are to master it. Paper works great for relating scale intervals, but not so well with topics related to timing. You have to hear, to understand most of the time. Considering this, I have broken down a few bars of chording onto a transcription so you can see the strumming breakdown and work out a specific example. What I am trying to do is just introduce the subject and break it down so that you can pick up guitar rhythms on your own after hearing them.

"The E chord is spelled out on the transcription across all six strings. The long V shape means strum across only the strings crossed by the V in the direction that the V is pointing on the indicated beat. Tap your foot 'one and two.'

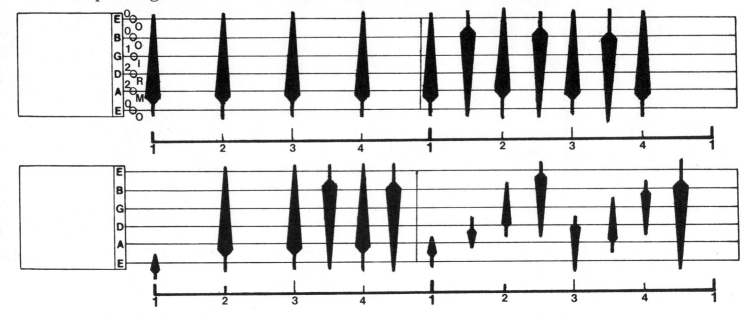

TRANSPOSING THE ROOT NOTE FRET

"You never know until you try. So try playing the blues scale — however you want — across the root note fret for these keys: E, open strings and twelfth fret, G third, A fifth, B seventh, D tenth, and E twelfth fret. Promise me you will go all the way up, then come all the way down at least twice in each key when you practice.

"I dare say that you will need an hour of practice with all of this coming down on you." The boy felt no need to talk because the air was perfectly warm as it passed by in an easy breeze. The old man was half-way down the roof hatch when he stopped to say, "Do you think that you understand about the blues scale, and the different techniques, Boy? In an hour we will go on from this point."

The boy stared out into the stars. "Well, I know that the twelve fret repeating pattern left by the pentatonic blues scale leaves seven chromatic steps unplayed. Each key has a blues root note fret, a unique position from the selection of twelve frets, where the notes from the blues scale can be played across the whole fret. This root note fret, where the basic lead guitar pattern is centered, takes place at the fifth and seventeenth fret for the key of A. In the key of E, the open strings and the twelfth fret are the centers. Now in the key of E the notes in the blues scale are E, G, A, B, D and in the key of A the notes are A, C, D, E, G. I guess that four notes are common to both scales and that the B note is unique to E blues and that the C note is unique to the A blues. Right, Old Man?"

A silence broke in on the boy, and as he turned to find the old man, he found himself alone.

10. Relative Degrees

I have good news, and I have bad news for you, Boy. The bad news is that you have to learn about a whole new scale."

"When is it going to end, Old Man?"

"Pretty soon, actually, Boy! You have to assimilate your technique applications so you can invent with them, but this is it for scales. Scales are only the keys to the car. Learning to use them is like a sphere within a sphere. There are ways to go through the scale, and there are ways to go through the scale, if you know what I mean. Just because you know where the thing is, *so what?*"

"So, what's with the new scale, Old Man. What's the good news about it?"

"Well, the good news is that it's identical to the blues scale." The boy stood transfixed like the desert sphinx letting the information sink in. "I'm telling you that it's identical in PATTERN but different in its POSITION. What is the name of the scale? *The relative scale.* What is it? It's a series of five notes which take their position at a fixed relative distance from each of the five blues scale degrees.

"Here is how the relative works. Picture the blues scale going up the low string starting in the key of A at the fifth fret. Keeping the interval pattern the same, pick up the whole deal and move it down three frets. These are the laws for positioning the relative scale for the key of A.

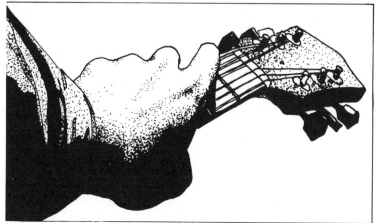

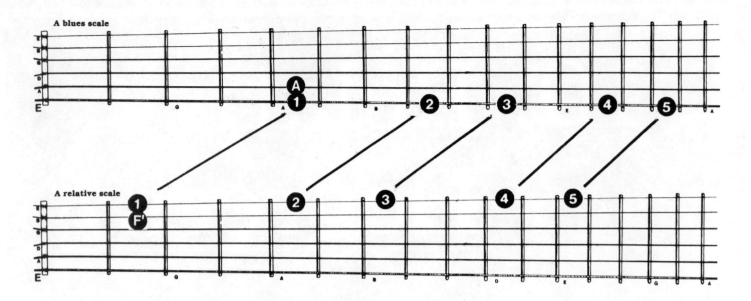

"Get serious here, Boy, because this has to do with whether you can cut it or not. Here is the pattern for the entire blues scale in A. Below it you will see the diagram for the relative scale in the same key. Look at the basic position for fingering across the fifth fret in the blues scale, and how it moves down to the second fret for the relative.

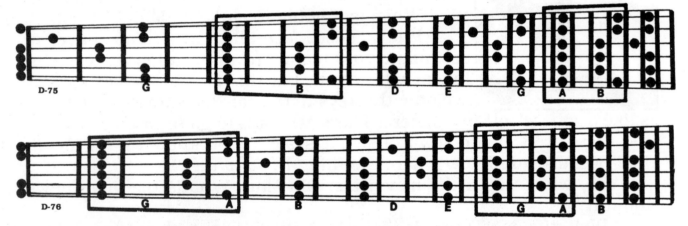

"The same thing happens in the key of E. You move the blues scale down three and you have the relative scale. Because the blues scale is centered around the open strings and the twelfth fret, the only practical center for the relative root note fret appears on the ninth fret. Here are the diagrams for the blues and relative scales in the key of E. Stare and compare.

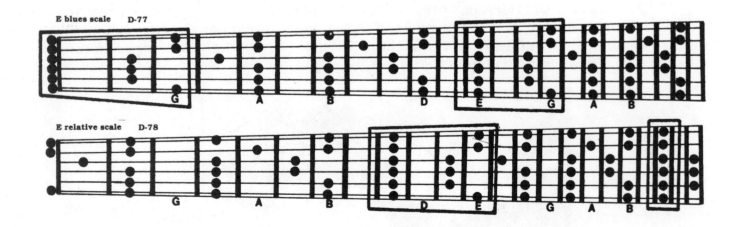

"Because the pattern of both considered scales is the same, the relative scale for the key of A is identical in every way to the blues scale in F sharp. The same thing goes for the relative scale in E and the blues scale in C sharp. Before we explore the consequences of double scale interaction, I want you to see this complex situation as something that is easy to understand. Don't forget, it is only the blues scale. You already know it. Run the transcription a couple of times and get a feel for this new relative scale.

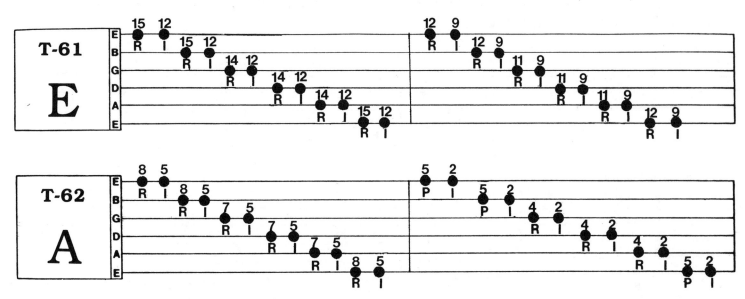

"The relationship between these two scales is easy to hear. The blues scale is brighter, commanding, and out front. The relative has that sort of misty, far away feeling. They are relatives to each other.

SOME THE SAME, SOME DIFFERENT

"This deal with two scales being the same in pattern but with one moved down in position three frets is no simple cookie. You're talking *two overlaying patterns.* The sticky wicket is this: two degrees from the relative scale are also common to the blues scale. Basing your point of view from the blues scale, the blues has five notes and the relative presents you with three more usable notes. Maybe these next diagrams will clear things up for you. The one on top is the relative scale in A, shown in circles. Here you have the relative scale between the second fret, the base for relative A, and the ninth fret.

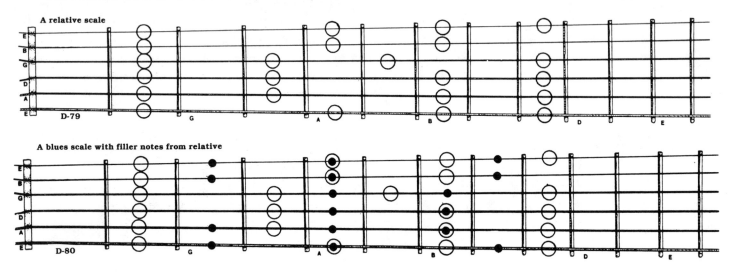

"The diagram on the bottom shows the blues scale in A along the root note fifth fret using black dots. The diagram on the top is superimposed on the bottom diagram so you can see which scale degrees are common and which are outstanding.

"We have five degrees in the blues scale. This we know. The relative comes along and gives us three more. Let me show you how these three supplementary notes fit in the first octave down in the key of E.

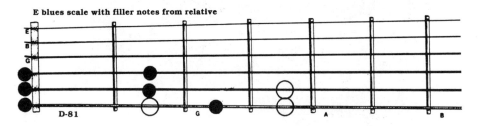

"Next I will show the whole fretboard for the key of E and A with the blues scale appearing in black dots and the three extra relative notes presented as circles.

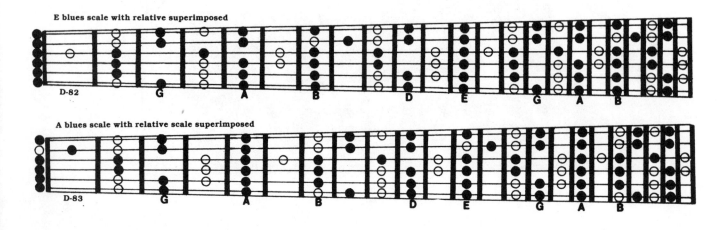

"The full implication of this takes a while to sink in. Don't forget — all of the fingering positions that you know from the blues scale also apply to the relative scale. Same deal with the index across the two thin strings on the fundamental fret. The technique bag applies to the relative just like the blues scale. The fact that the relative is three down keeps sneaking up behind you and, smack, you begin to see! One secret is to 'see' a blues position three down. Another is to 'see' the extra relative notes immediately around the blues pattern you are using so you can tap them. Just keep bringing the blues down three. Eventually you will see the rules.

"The last diagram was sort of crazy with dots, so let's cut it down to something we can live with. The top diagram runs our blues root note fret in A. The bottom diagram shows you how the three extra relative notes appear in clusters around our basic position. Mind you — these clusters are comprised of the same three notes.

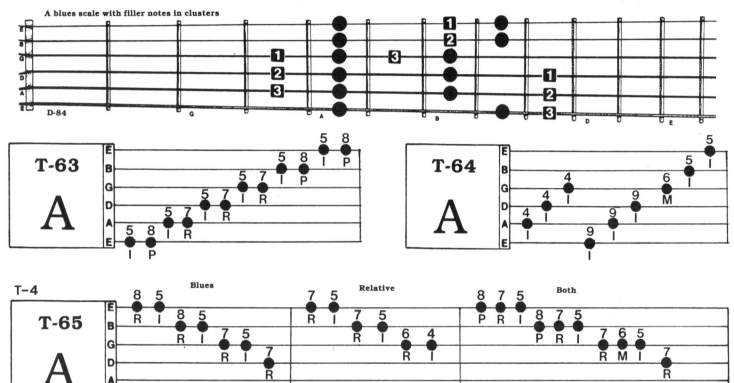

A blues scale with filler notes in clusters

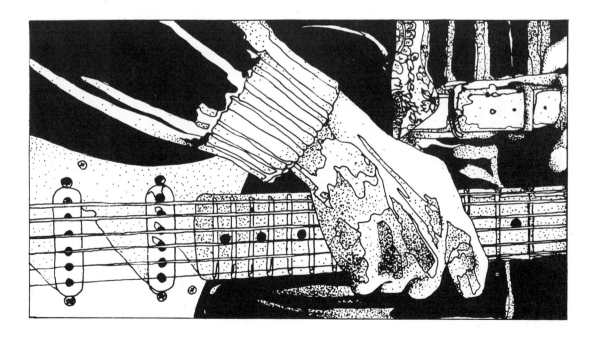

"Now listen up! We have these two scales — the blues and the relative. I know we have talked a lot about scales, but for right now, just think of the blues scale as number one and the relative scale as number two. That is pretty much how you will play them from now on. Now check this out — we are not talking scale pattern now. We are talking concept of approach. There are three different working ways in which we can approach playing with these two scales.

BLUE SUNGLASSES

"Your blues sunglasses are to be worn when you are thinking only of employing the blues scale for your lead guitar work. You know the jive five, especially across the root note fret. It's a way of thinking, Boy. Only the blues scale.

RED SUNGLASSES

"Hey, baby, when you're seeing red you are playing exclusively in the relative scale. You have decidedly moved the blues scale down three and you are running your game using relative degrees only.

LIGHT BLUE SUNGLASSES

"When you put these on you are still seeing blues scale, but you know where the extra red relative notes are located, and you can throw them in as you will. You can switch glasses as often as you wish, and how and when you do is a function of your talent. Study and develop yourself, Boy. Here is a transcription that will tune you in on the different color glasses:

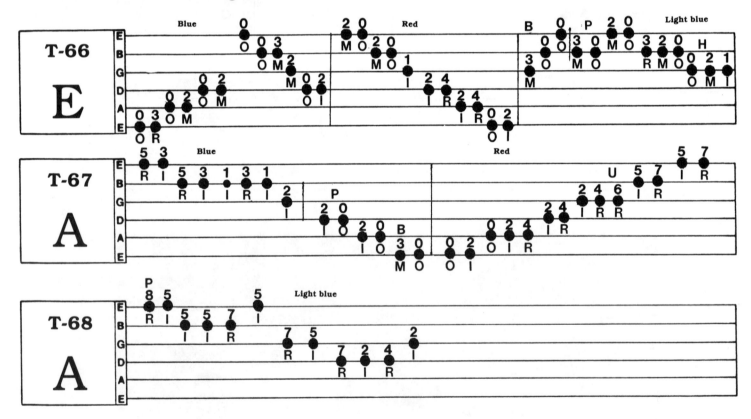

"Now practice your rainbow, Boy. Next we will take a closer look at each of those three extra relative notes."

11. Symbols To Understand

A symbol is a token of identity which is verified by comparison. Mankind has used symbols ever since the dawn of the species. The might of the dominant ape stood as a symbol of territorial right. Sometimes symbols were used as a mark of ownership, and sometimes they stood as universal characters which told of things known. Once overpopulation set in, symbols no longer had to be obscure, but could take their form right out of real life. The guitar is by far the most symbolic of all modern instruments. The blues musicians that sang at the middle class through their radios in the forties and fifties were symbols of menace. The guitar stood for freewheeling good times to the kids that had to stay home. To formal musicians, the guitar often stood as the symbol of a popular instrument, not worthy of their stuffy consideration. To many a factory worker it was a symbol of hope, a key to break out of a regimented lifestyle. To those who walked in the front door of the barrelhouse it was a symbol of time spent without worry — a chance to get beyond immediate problems. Here are the symbols we are going to use, Boy:

| Star | Moon | Triangle | Diamond | Square |

"Each one will be assigned to a specific note from the chromatic scale. Now let's gear ourselves up with facts. The chromatic is all twelve half-steps between the octaves. Twelve is the full number. We have chosen five of these twelve as the degrees of our basic scale — the blues scale. We introduced the pentatonic relative scale, and this brought three new independent degrees into the picture. Now, if we add the five from the blues with the three from the relative, we get eight. Eight out of twelve — that's not bad, eh, Boy? The three extra notes that the relative presents will each get their own symbol.

"Now in addition to these three notes, I will also show you two common chromatic filler notes. With these two filler notes added to our eight, we will be up to ten. That leaves two notes from our twelve-note master scale unaccounted for. These two notes are rarely used, but will be identified.

"Here is how the symbol game is spelled out along the bottom octave of the guitar in the key of E along the low E string. The black dots with numbers are the blues scale in E, you remember, E, G, A, B and D. Each symbol has one certain note which it identifies.

E blues scale with symbols to understand

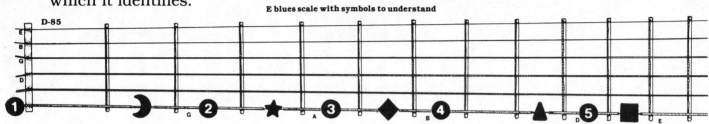

"The unmarked first fret note, the F note for the key of E, is rarely used because it is so close to the powerful tonic center. The second unmarked position, the eighth fret or C note, is actually the flatted sixth that is used in some minor scale modes. It is rarely used for blues.

"The first three symbols we want to check out are the three relative degrees that aren't in the blues scale. Shall we start working, Boy?

THE STAR ★

"The star is the third of the major scale and is a primary component of the major triad. Stare at the diagram until you 'see' the whole E chord bar across all six strings. You will find the rest of the major chord, the first and the fifth, to be in the blues scale.

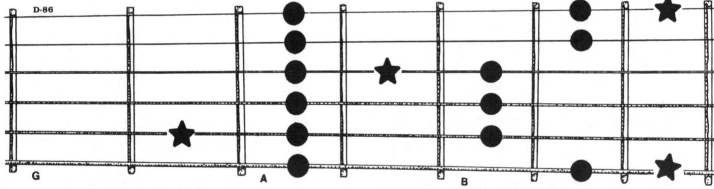

"Check out each of the stars separately. It's so much fun to figure out riffs using the blues scale around each of these guys. We've got it all here, Boy—High, Middle, Low. The first string star is above the basic box and I have seen that flatted third, three above the tonic, get bent to sound this star. The star on the third string is used in the common basic chord position. What more can I say? It's easy to play with the middle after the index is centered on the root note fret. The star on the fifth string can be played by sliding the index down from the note above it or by grabbing it from below. The star on the low E string is an important bass note. Here are some short examples to help you understand the star's use:

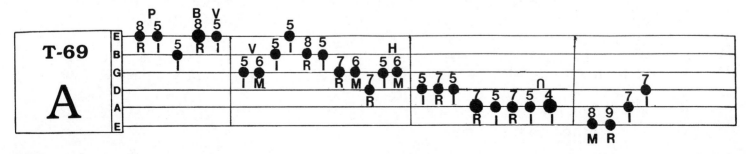

THE MOON 🌙

"The half-moon symbol is actually the second of the major scale, two frets above the tonic. The moons on the E strings are sweet because of the easy whole-step position above the root note fret. The moon on the third string is on that odd fret right below the root note fret. The fourth string moon is reached by stepping up. The moon note is a beauty! It can add such a nice melodic touch to the direct slant of the blues scale. Here is a slice of the pie. Eat up.

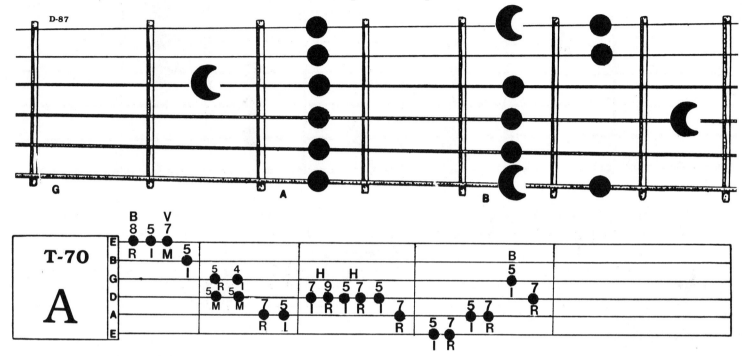

THE TRIANGLE ▲

"The triangle is the symbol for the sixth of the major scale. This is one of our extra relative notes and works with the star and moon to complete our study of the individual relative scale degrees. Of the three triangles that you see, it is the one on the second string that is the most widely used because of its optimal position a whole-step above the root note fret. At this position it works hand-in-glove with the other notes around the 'index across the two thin strings' position which is held across the fifth fret. Know it, Boy!

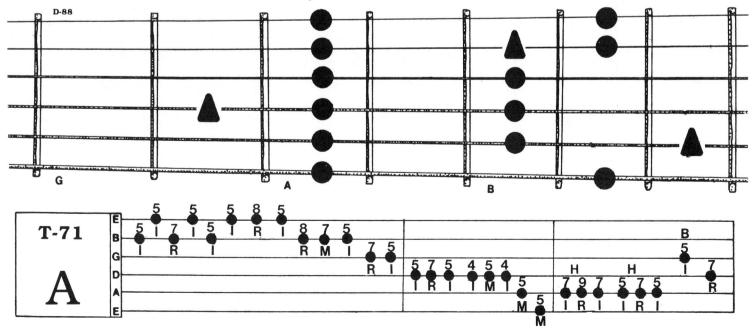

THE DIAMOND

"Here is a great chromatic filler which is primarily used as a quick step between the fourth and fifth of the major scale. Get to know the diamond between the fourth and the fifth of the major on the fifth string, and also on the third string. The diamond is often employed in a move to resolve the fifth as a lead-in note. It can also be used as a smart roller over the fourth degree. Play every note of the transcription. Read it closely. Then play it twice and the clouds will clear.

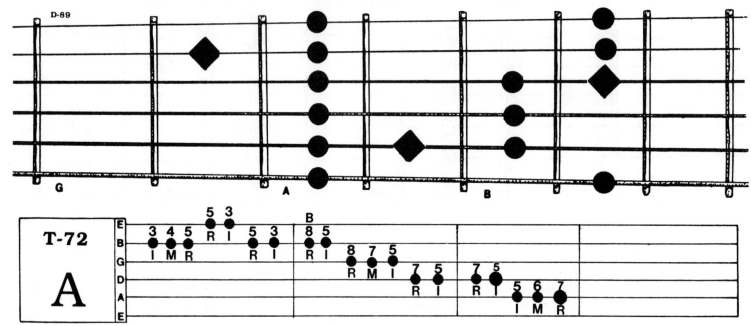

THE SQUARE

"The square is sort of an out-note. You can use it for filling in runs that come up from under the tonic. It is actually the seventh of the major scale which is known as the leading tone because of its tendency to resolve up to the tonic. I have combined both filler notes together for this transcription:

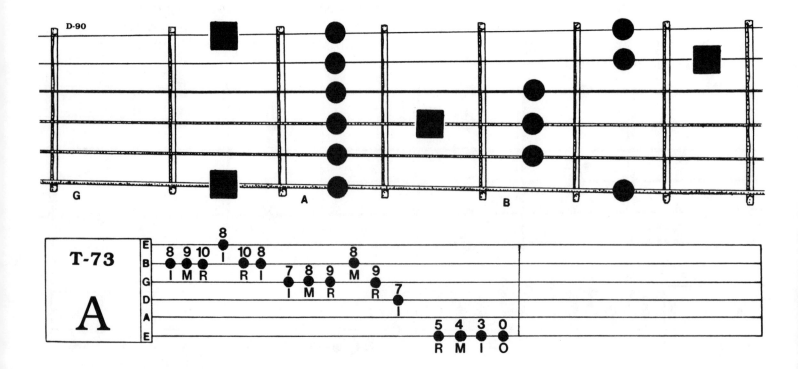

"You definitely have your hands full with the symbols, considering that you have a guitar case full of technique notes that you have not mastered. But that's alright, Boy. You see the picture, now. I'll run you down one more time. Please read carefully. Key of E.

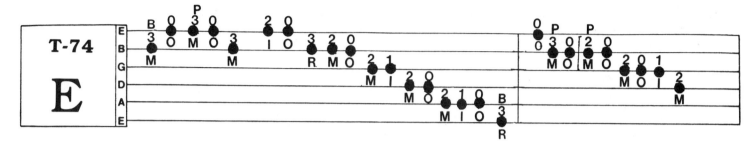

"Without even knowing it, we seem to have arrived at the blues! You have a lot behind you now, Boy. The chords, the major and blues fingerings, the technique review, the relative, the symbols to understand — everything is coming together now. The transcriptions with the symbols were windows that you can use to see into blues licks. They are short and not exhaustive, but that riff, that one hook, that singular idea that is so much fun to do. That is what is in the making with these symbol transcriptions. We started out with a lot of stuff that didn't have that much to do with the blues, but you know now that I want you to think in terms of the blues scale. The relative can also be used, but eventually you end up in orbit around the blues scale. It is good to know the major, especially for reference. But as far as playing blues guitar straight out in the major scale, well, I don't do it much.

"One thing I don't want you to forget in your quest for the perfect blues riff are the all-familiar primary notes. The tonic is the first of all scales and the fourth and fifth are common to the major, blues and relative scales. The best riffs are simple in structure. Knowing what note to go to is more important than rushing through the scale to nowhere. You are after a sound, Boy.

"Now concentrate and try this double triplet that is built onto the single triplet model we studied a while back. First I'll show the single triplet, then the double which has both a moon and a triangle in their makeup. Can you find them?"

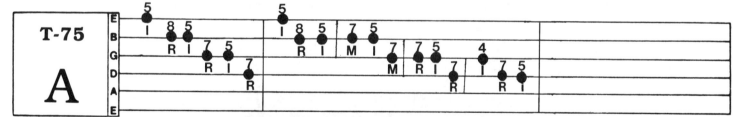

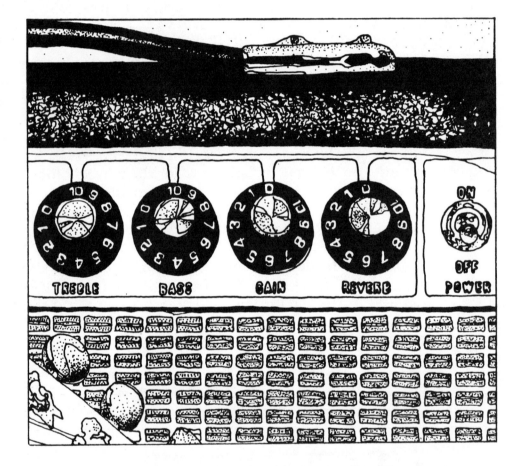

12. Hit The Bins

ooks like we stayed up all night again, Old Man.'' The sun was lighting up the eastern horizon as the stars slowly gave way to the light blues of the morning sky.

"Come and follow me, Boy,'' the old man said as he headed for the stairway with the boy close behind. "Everything is down in the basement, Boy. You have gone far enough into the paper chase. You can only talk about it to a certain degree. There is nothing wrong with studying all of the positions, scales and so forth. But that is only half of the game. One half cannot substitute for the other — no matter how hard you try.''

The old wooden stairs creaked as the old man kicked a door open into a basement room. The old man walked directly up to a table that had an old-style record changer and a huge pile or record albums. "Go ahead and pull up a chair, Boy, and check out some of these blues albums.'' The boy's eyes opened wide to take in all of the information. "Sometimes it's hard to believe that these albums really exist. Here, hold them in your hands.'' The old man handed the boy a full stack of about fifty albums and then went about his business of preparing the record player. "Check out each record jacket carefully as you look at each one. For starters, I want you to know that BLUES RECORDS DO EXIST! This is no lost art. The records in your hands can send the blues right into this very room. It's a miracle, I tell you. You were *born* into the age of miracles, Boy, so sometimes you have to be reminded of the incredible potential that waits right before your eyes, right at your finger tips.

"You know, it's hard to get your bearing today. Whenever I listen to the FM radio today, it has an over-kill of steady, non-stop, fast moving music which seems to just go on and on. So much of it seems created just for its own sake. No rhyme or reason — just the newest tunes, and more ads. Don't get me wrong. I enjoy listening to it when they hit on a good song. The thing that bothers me is the lack of real life urgency, the lack of sincerity that sets in when you move away from the human aspects and employ only technical means."

"Where did you get all of these albums, Old Man? All of the names from history you told me about are here — all in one stack of albums."

"I bought them all in regular record stores, right over the counter. There is a method I employ whenever I am in a record shop. I call it 'hit the bins'. Just walk through all of the latest hit propaganda on your way to the record bin marked BLUES. Locate the first and last record, and one by one, go through each and every album that the place has. Pick out a few dozen that you want and buy them. Then go on to the next store and do the same thing."

"Sure, Old Man. How can I afford that?"

"The music is on that record, Boy. The BLUES is on that record! Mow lawns, stand on your head, beg your mother for pennies. Just buy that record and walk out — get the sequence." The old man opened a closet door to show the boy hundreds of albums lining the shelves. "All blues, Boy, only blues." The boy swallowed hard and bobbed his head as his eyes surveyed the archives. "Some stores have a lot more Blues records than others, but almost all will have some. You have to ask where they are located in most stores because they put them way in the back. The stores don't sell them as fast as hit records. I'm trying to tell you that the history of the blues is waiting in a record bin for you. Just keep looking in different stores, and after a while, you will find one place that has what you need.

"In 1877, Thomas Edison started the whole thing off when he made a crude recording onto tin foil of himself singing *Mary Had A Little Lamb.* Even I don't have that one, but I have the rest!" The old man reached over to the tone arm and held it a fraction of an inch over a spinning record. "If you listen to enough of these things, eventually you get to know the styles from the different years. Don't forget, by the time the modern rock groups came around, there was already fifty long years of blues recording development. Anyway, the reason I brought you down here is to hear the old blues."

The needle made its way to the record and was playing the blank grooves before the first song. "I like my record players cheap, Boy. It gives the records that real touch at high volumes." The old man laughed as the boy shook his head in frowned disbelief.

The speakers in the corner of the room started to blast out an old blues standard with so much force that the boy had to raise his voice to ask, "Who is it?"

"It's Elmore James playing *Dust My Broom.*" The old man didn't have to say anything more. He could tell that the boy was getting the message. After the song the old man lifted up the tone arm.

"That was incredible, Old Man. I have never heard that much drive in a guitarist before! I can't believe what I just heard!"

"That's okay, Boy. You have had three minutes of the other half that I was talking about. Remember that I said you could not substitute one for the other? Now you know. Diagrams are fine in their place, but the record opens you up to the real thing. All that you really have to know about the guitar is a general overview and a few specific examples. The records have all of the variety and raw inventions that you need to get a head full of ideas. What I want to do now, Boy, is just sit back and listen to a couple of hours of blues guitar. Don't just dream away into the music. Be aware of the tempo, the phrasing of the licks, the chord change, the form that the guy is using. Figure out how the beat is divided and what instruments are in the band. Check out the bridge in a song, if there is one, and listen to the voice as it moves over the twelve bars. Try to figure out what it is you like about a song, or dislike for that matter. Listen to the words and take them in. Count the bars and

wait for the resolution. Get ready for that first bar to kick in right after the twelfth. There is nothing more to say, except, here comes the blues in all its variation!''

The old man set up a large stack of records on the automatic turntable and sat back to listen. The records went by like long trains, each leaving a distinct impression after the last car rumbled away. Over the hours the boy heard the music from every period of blues history. Finally the old man reached over to turn the volume way down so he could talk over the music. ''That Lightning Hopkins is something, eh, Boy?''

''Yeah. He likes that slow empty-time pause, doesn't he?''

''How about that B. B. King. He walks that single line on the thin strings a lot. I have an interview with him from *Guitar Player Magazine* someplace here. I have every copy ever printed in the closet next to the records.''

The boy raised his eyebrows and simply said, ''I believe you do!''

''Each record is a whole story in itself. Listen closely to Leadbelly and you will hear that lonely field holler rearing its head. When the Robert Johnson record is on I can think of nothing else but the sheer tension that he creates. His voice is snarled, his acoustic guitar's a steely edge that is impossible to forget. The delta guitarists have a sense of rhythm that they carry out onto the strings. The variety is staggering when you compare one artist to another. Remember those classic singers that we heard, Boy? Wasn't that clarinet player funny? You know, he is using pretty much the same game as that old guy with the lone guitar and harmonica. When Robert Nighthawk sings about going down to Eli's, he does it using the first, the fourth and the fifth.''

Just the reference to dry scale degrees sent the boy into another frame of mind. The old man shook his head slowly. ''Hard to believe, but true, Boy. All of that study we did really does apply to this music. It seems too much removed to have anything to do with it, but that is the great thing about it. Remember I told you 'quiet time first, then party time'. Now you've had a taste of both.

"Go back to the record for the true grit, Boy. Fortunately for the blues record buyer, there are many composite blues albums with several artists on one album. There are also several small record companies that carry the blues torch forward by remembering the past. I have one album called 'Roots of Rock' where all of the recordings are from between 1927 and 1930. It has Charley Patton, Skip James, Tommy Johnson and Blind Blake, along with eight others, all on the same album. Another of my favorites is a double-album called 'The Story of the Blues' which is divided up into four sections: The Origin of the Blues with cuts by Mississippi John Hurt, Blind Lemon Jefferson and Texas Alexander; Blues and Entertainment with Barbeque Bob and Bessie Smith; The Thirties, Urban and Rural Blues with Robert Johnson, Peetie Wheatstraw; and the last section called World War II and After with Big Bill Broonzy, Elmore James and Brownie McGhee. Over forty artists are represented on this double-record set. This is just to give you an idea of what your resources are right this minute, Boy. The funny thing is that you had to have it spelled out for you before you knew what you had going for yourself.

"My teachings aren't over yet, Boy. There are still many more singular facts and concepts that I want to present to you. I waited to show you the records until I thought you were ready. But now, the cats are out of the bag, and you know where to find the deep fresh water well when you need it. In a while I will show you how to actually work with the record to pick up any riff you want. You will go on, Boy. You will have your day alone in the sun. Take my advice and get a few records of your own. I asked you to play that blues scale one hundred times because I knew that the next day you would know it if you did. These records work the same way. They grow on you until, when you're alone, you will hear them play in your mind. You'll be able to actually figure stuff out right in your head waiting in the elevator to get to your floor. Nobody knows but you, Boy."

The old man grabbed a guitar and quietly kneeled down in front of the record player's speaker and quickly tuned up the six strings to match the recording that was playing. "Now get your hour of practice with the record today, Boy. I tuned this guitar so you can play in A along with this recording of Juke Boy Bonner called *I'm A Blues Man*. Now, I want you to play this song over and over until you've lost it, Boy. Get narrow. Don't worry about the closet full of records. Just play with this one song. You should center your lead out of the fifth fret position for the root note fret. You will use A, D and E for chords, the three fat strings open."

The old man turned up the volume a bit and handed the guitar to the boy, setting the tone arm down on the first cut of the record. "Play that blues scale right with that cat. Run your root note fret, Boy."

The boy played as if it were his first time. The phrasing of the note took on immediate importance where it had none in cold practice. "Now, go down to the second fret and center yourself in the relative scale for A." The boy's hand moved down, his face frozen in concentration. "Now go to the fifth, Boy. Get that low E string. Now come into the first bar with a tonic note singing. You are on your own, Boy."

The old man headed for the door going up to the kitchen. He could hear the boy's guitar clearly mixed with the recording as the notes melted together. The old man sat quietly on the outside porch listening to the music as it made its way outside into the morning light. After an hour, the second song on the album began to play, and the old man knew that the boy was asleep.

13. Twelve To One

Same thing as an apple tree, those records are, Boy.'' The door to the basement room slammed open from the kick of the old man. ''You see hundreds of beautiful red apples, you take in the whole tree, then you pick just one apple and eat it.''

The boy shook the sleep out of his head. ''Sure, Old Man. Just like apples.''

''You just got vaccinated with the blues, Boy,'' the old man remarked as he lifted the tone arm off the middle of the turning record. ''You have to study them one at a time. We have the stack of records all together, but the time periods in which they were recorded are grossly different. The people who made the recordings are individuals — each with their own. The blues form is the constant, but the manisfestation of musical element springs from the artist's talent and the particulars that affected a single recording date. The performer's background always comes out in the wash. To make things even deeper, many artists recorded over a span of decades. You have to ask 'who, when, where and what' in order to fill in all the pieces. Some album covers give the low-down and some don't.

''Never get to the point where you are not listening. You can study a recording just like you can study a scale. Just like a zoom lens — you can take in the whole thing and see its form or you can pick out a riff that you like. A teacher tries to organize things into general terms. A performer's goal is a unique style, including single hooks, moves and textures. Each guy has a personal bag of tricks that are trademarks. This could be a certain turn in a vocal technique, or a type of ending or intro. It all depends on which apple you pick. The subtle stuff is what makes a record stand out. It could be the command of a falsetto technique, where the voice is artificially forced to go into an upper range. I have a Leadbelly record where he sings acappella without accompaniment. That means without guitar, to you, Boy. Maybe a singer uses flighty grace notes to make a distinctive style. How about a brilliant flight of fantasy towards the end of an instrumental solo, formally called a cadenza, which returns a strict tempo when the wheels eclipse. The band's drummer might use a flam — a single stroke on the snare drum. One guy might just talk a line over the thump-thump tonic bass. Next thing you know, you have some big band fragmenting, modifying and combining themes over each other. You heard it all. Time to get back to the kitchen table for awhile, Boy."

The old man and the boy walked up to the kitchen where a small cassette machine and a stack of unused diagram paper awaited. "The guitar is set up to play blues in E as far as I'm concerned, Boy. You have that basic fret right there at the open strings. The first, the fourth and the fifth major triad are easily accessible and the blues scale works even across the fifth and seventh fret on the three low strings. The key of A is the second key, with its open tonic string being the fifth. The first, fourth and fifth of A are also readily accessible. The fifth fret root can be worked from under and above, with the fifth and seventh fret position for E moving up to ten and twelve. The key of G can be played sliding the root note fret for A down two frets. The keys of B and C can be centered by moving the key of A picture up two and three frets respectively. The key of D root note fret is easily pictured by moving down the twelfth fret E root note fret, which you have practiced. So we study these two keys — E and A — and you move your fret to get others.

"Now I want you to think in terms of completing the blues all the way through in a repeating twelve-bar pattern. Don't think in terms of one bar as much as playing it one through twelve, then twelve to one.

FIRST, FOURTH AND FIFTH CHORDS

"Once more, Boy. For the key of E the three chords are E, A and B. For the key of A it goes A, D and E. All together, we only have to look at four chords to cover all that we need for both of our keys. Here are those four chords with an extra B seventh chord thrown in for good luck:

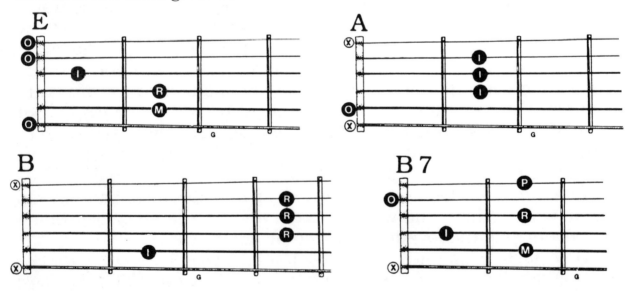

RHYTHM RIFF

"The basic bottom riff for the blues guitarist, one used by all rhythm guitarists, involves a tap-on above the fifth of the E chord in its basic position. This riff uses a movable pattern to convey its message. The transcription is broken down into four parts. Study all of them closely. Try to make them roll when you play them. A word on that fourth one: this is the movable guy. The transcription is short, but don't let that fool you. The secret to playing good rock and roll guitar is learning how to push the movable around, and run your blues scale around the root note fret. Sooooooo.

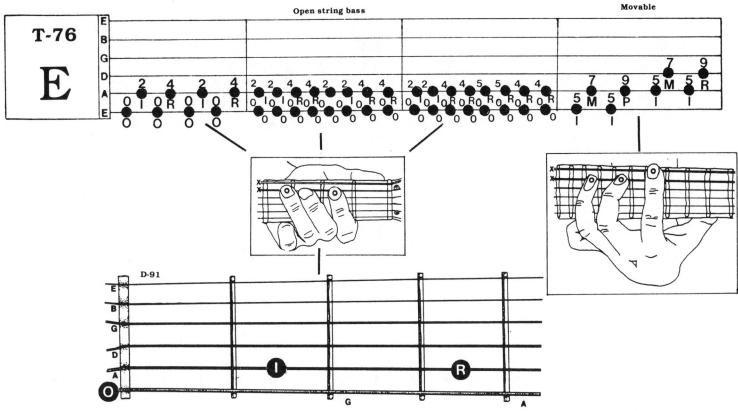

ONCE THRU THEN TWICE THRU

"The time is now to go through the twelve-bar. You have to start somewhere and this is it. Don't worry about variations. We will get to them, too. But right now, work with this transcription. Go through it once just to get the fingering and positions down. Then try it again. When you think you are ready to try your run all the way through, just press off the pause button on the recorder and you will have a live mike. No more questions will be accepted after you press the pause button. No more will be explained either. Good luck, Boy.

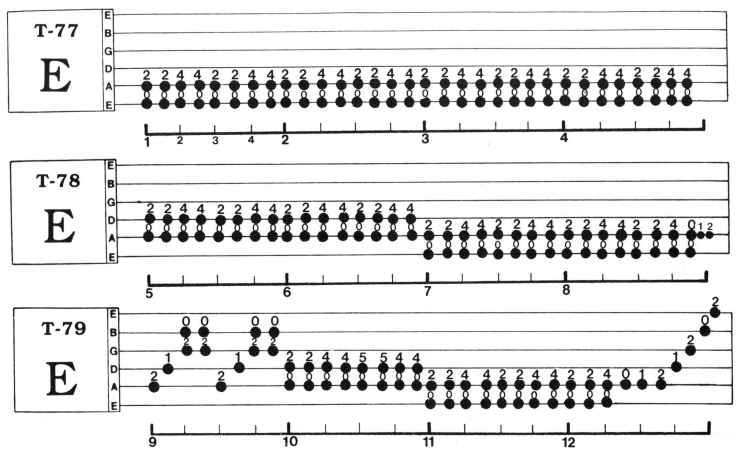

"Think about two things: which bar you are on and which chord is going to come around next. After you play along with a couple more records, you will feel the changes in your blood. Now, here is another way through the E blues. You use that movable bar rhythm riff for this one. I threw in a high position for the E-based position at the seventh and eighth bar, but this was just to show you the position so you would know that it was there. To simplify the diagram I didn't double up the dots like I did on the first one. Play it however you want.

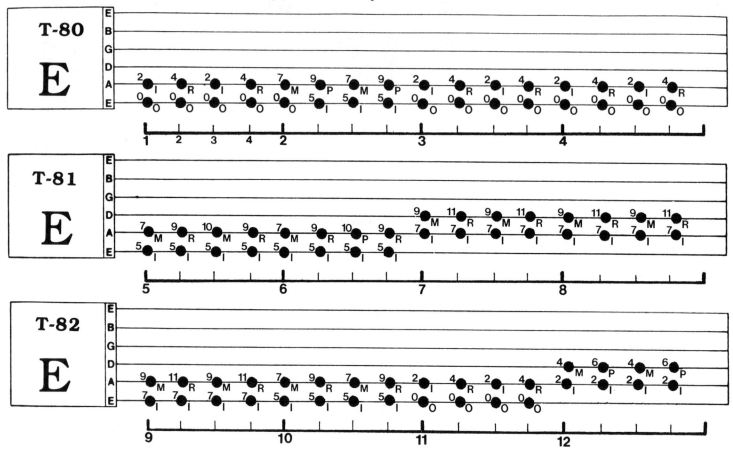

"Now I want to go over a few variations of the rhythm riff using open strings. Check out the transcription. Look for sixth string and fifth string-based riffs.

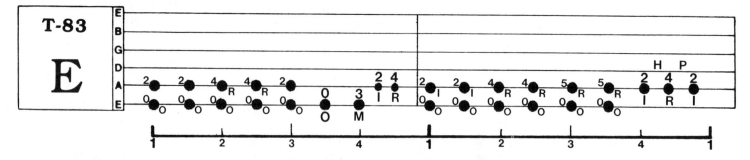

"Here is another way through that gives you an idea of where the first, the fourth and the fifth triads take place. Please note the use of the E seventh chord for the fourth bar. This is a distinctive blues technique which you will hear on many recordings. Make your chord position once for each place then pluck the notes out of the chord formation.

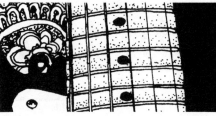

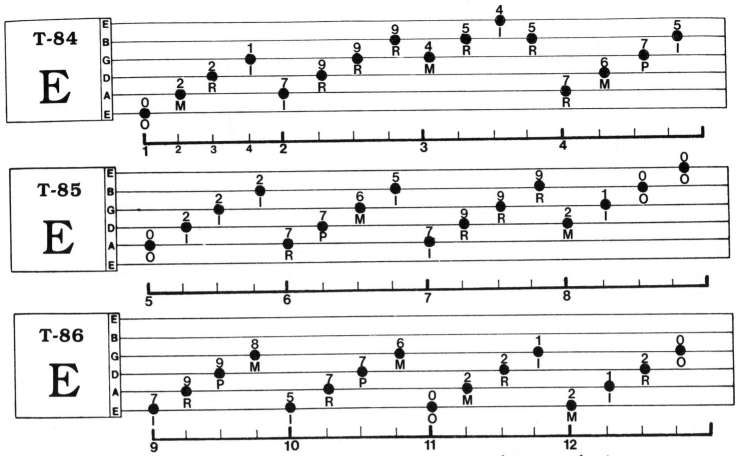

"This next way through is in the key of A. Once again, this example gives you a range of positions that I want you to know. When you play actual songs you probably won't hop around this much because you will establish yourself around one center.

"Anyway, practice until you think you can keep your time all the way through and then we will tape twelve bars. That should keep you sharp because that tape doesn't lie.

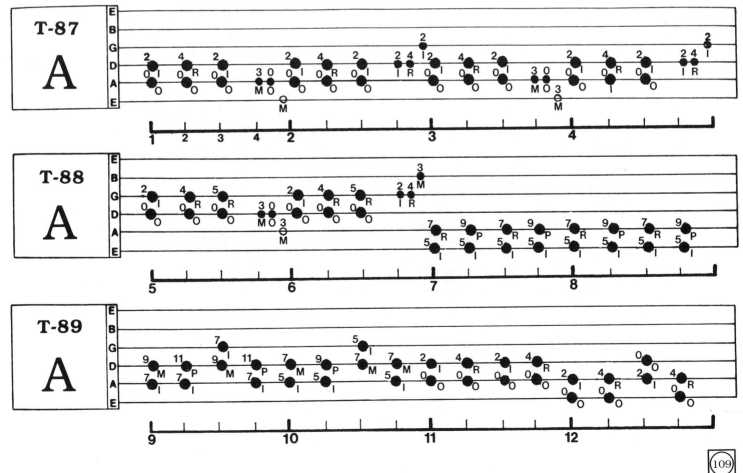

"Now let's go through one in the key of A that works around broken chords. Of course, you can strum these chords to any rhythm that you want. Up strokes are very effective because of the accent on the upper strings. This should be revealing.

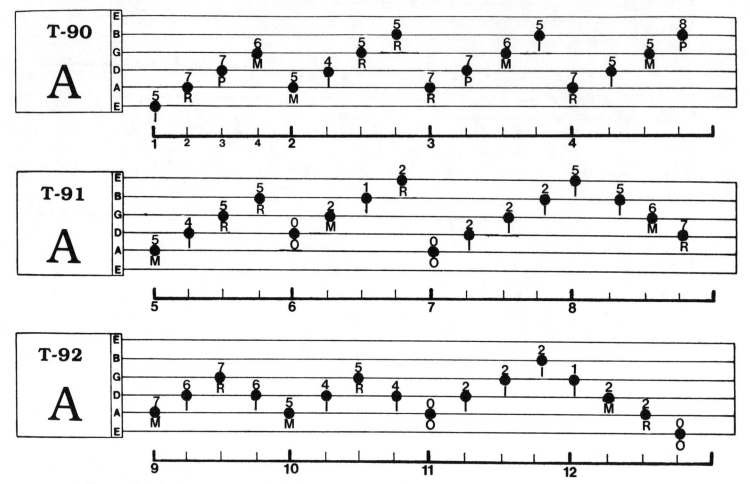

"I want you to use your head to mix and match all of the positions that you have seen in the transcriptions.

"We have been looking at the underlying structure that holds together the momentum of a song. Next we are going to look at the bass line and examine it to find what we will. Strive to find that point where you feel like you are in control of the music. This is especially important when you are performing alone. Ride over it. Push yourself to that point where you are ahead of the beat in your mind. Then you will have that extra card to play. When the key points roll around, you will come down with a riff that is phrased so sweet, everybody will immediately know that you are for real.

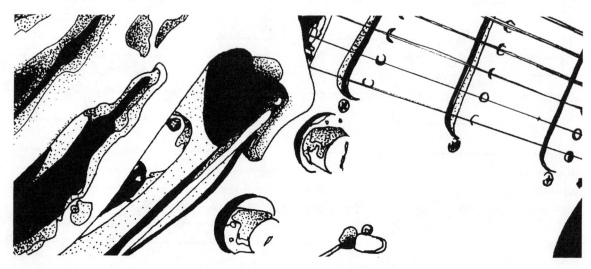

14. The Bottom

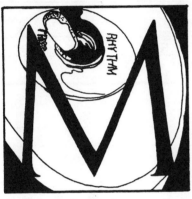

Musicians have to think dimensionally. You have to consider all of the diverse factors that constitute the makeup of a song, and try to put it down across the board on your instrument. The old solo delta guys were interesting to watch. They would play the chords to time, then they would stop and play a few notes of lead, and then go into a pounding bass line that put the thing back on the beat. That's what the bass is for -- holding down the bottom.

"The common electric bass has the same notes as the bottom four strings of the regular six-string, E, A, D, G, but is tuned an octave lower. The bass lines I am going to present should be played on the bottom strings of the six-string, but there is no reason why you couldn't play the transcription using a bass.

"We can save a little set-up time this time around because the centers around which our changes take place have already been established. Tap your foot as you go, Boy. You have to start looking at it from some angle, so we will start with this twelve-bar example in E. Note how the single note line works directly with the beat indicator line. After you go through it once, try doubling each note in the transcription, using a subdivision beat.

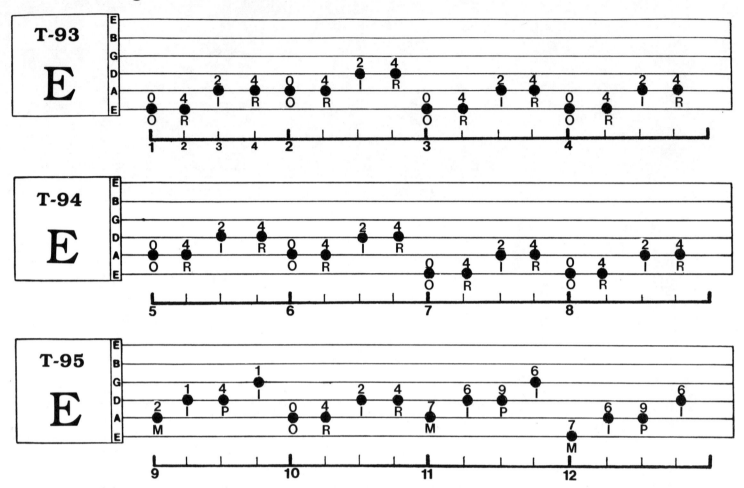

"Pretty nice. One good thing about bass lines is that you can see and hear them coming around to the resolve. This makes it easy to get the feel for them. What I have next for you are two variations for the E position using the low string. You can also move it to the A string and use it for that position. To go to the fifth, or B chord position, you just move up the A position two frets. This can take place on the fifth string at the second fret, or the sixth string at the seventh fret. The B is definitely the odd pattern, but if you study it, you can come up with your own way to work things out. Here are those two variations. The first one uses grace notes as lead-ins to the basic steps. Ring that octave E at the second fret/fourth string. The second example uses a descending passage. Hit each note with conviction, making sure that the first count is right on time.

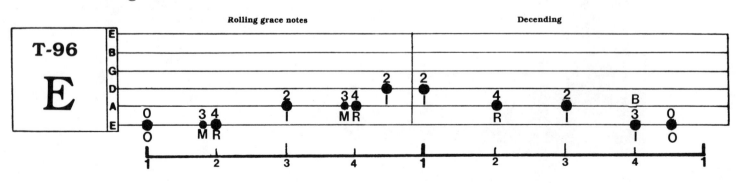

"Now I get to show you the walking bass. This move takes a single four-count bar to ascend, and then another full bar to descend down to set up another cycle starting at the third bar. Since it takes two bars for a complete cycle, the line can go up and down twice in the first four bars around the E center. During the fifth and sixth bars, it makes one cycle in the A-based position. Then it goes back to E for another turn during bars seven and eight. Because of the number of chord changes in the final four bars, there is no room for the two-bar cycle, so the line rolls through single ascending bars until the first comes back.

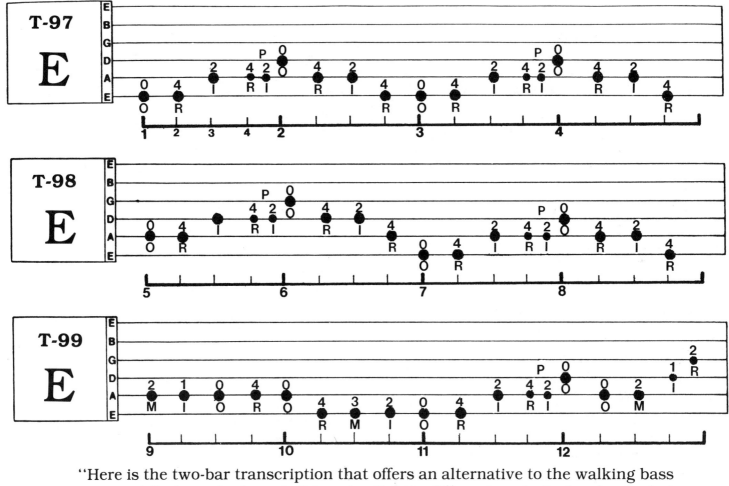

"Here is the two-bar transcription that offers an alternative to the walking bass arrangement that you just used. It is only slightly different, so look closely at what you are doing.

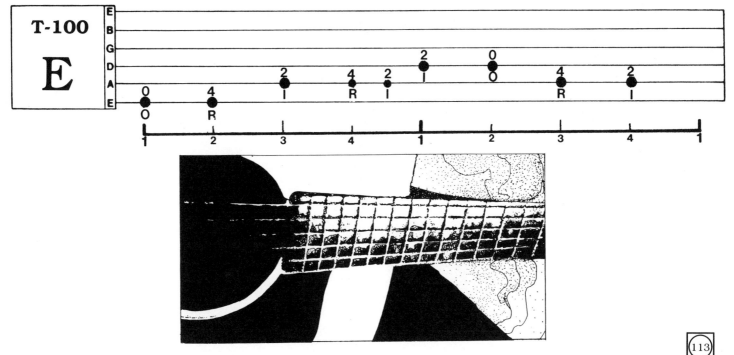

"To play in the key of A you just move your fundamental note around the A, D and E centers. Here is an abbreviated transcription which will give you a passage through each of the three centers for A.

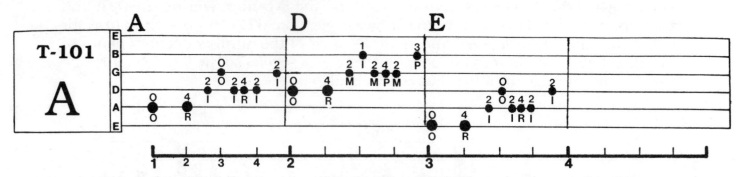

"Bass lines are easy to pick up off the record compared to chords and lead work. Just keep listening and now and then you will hear something that is really unique. After a while the whole thing gets down to bits and pieces, and throwing things together into a full twelve bars. For example, here is a transcription of only the seventh and eighth bars in the key of E to show you a minor lead-in to the resolution in B:

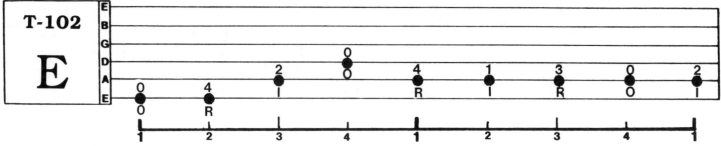

"The bass line can be mixed and matched with rhythm patterns. Bass always works close to the chord, weaving its pattern in, around and through the first, third and fifth of the major scale. Don't be fooled into thinking that bass guitar is simple. It can get very sophisticated, just as it can get very basic. One thing about the blues, Boy, it's not always flashing and dynamic. You will learn this the first time you are depended on to form a full rhythm with just one guitar. Right now it might seem like you have too many positions to learn. But after a while you will want more to give you variations, and you will find that the board does have its limitations. The basic rule is: grind through at all costs. That will make the high points sound all the better when they finally do come to the surface. When things seem down, just concentrate on that bottom. You build momentum from the regular beat, those regular finger snaps."

15. The Line

Aline consists of motion, the up and down movement of a series of notes, and rhythm, the long or short duration of those notes. The word line is usually taken to mean melody, but we will stretch the meaning to encompass any passage, long or short, that is singular and played over the beat. A line is said to have *ascending* motion if it is moving up in pitch, or *descending* motion if it is moving down. *Conjunct* motion is used to describe a line that is moving up or down in a progression of small steps. *Disjunct* describes a line that moves up or down in large intervals.

"The word *homophonic* is used to describe music that has only one melody line played over a chord sequence, whereas *polyphonic* means playing more than one line at the same time. This second category is generally known as counterpoint. The use of two lines makes for a complex system of possibilities [Appendix 6]. The most popular double line technique used by a blues guitarist is singing and playing a line simultaneously. This is a very old and very effective device for those who really know their guitar.

"As its core, the blues is an improvised art. Most great blues artists reached their level of proficiency by just starting young and learning the tricks one by one, until, one day, it was evident that they had evolved their own characteristic style. Because great artists assimilate a whole blues vocabulary, they no longer need raw outside input to get great inventive ideas. They already know enough. The student's situation is different. You have to get familiar by playing the riffs, rolling with the twelve-bar over and over. I also advise you, Boy, to take time out to really analyze new methods, or even those which you already 'know.' Breaking down a chord for inspective study is called harmonic analysis. These are fancy words for figure it out, Boy. You don't have to go in so far that you won't use what you find. But when you stop and analyze what notes you are using, it brings the fretboard out into the cleansing light of day. This isn't some passing fancy, Boy. This instrument will stay the same as it is for the rest of your life. The sooner you bring your playing out of the shadows, the sooner you'll master the fretboard. Strive to find universal methods that can be applied to your playing.

SUBSTITUTION

The replacement of one note for another in a passage is an effective common practice. Maybe if I give you an example, you can learn to recognize the technique and use it on your own. The next transcription takes a typical blues riff which starts on the tonic and, in the second part of the transcription, substitutes a minor third blue note for the original tonic.

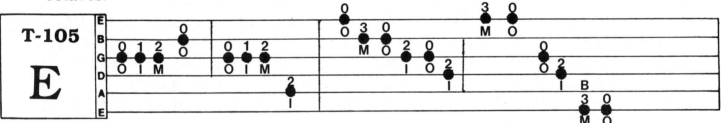

"Here is another simple substitution which uses the second instead of the fifth of the major scale. The third section of the transcription uses the upper second."

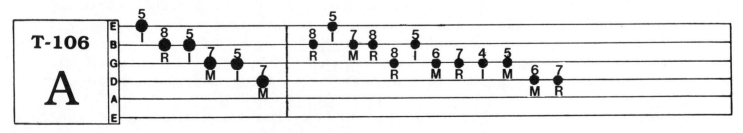

"Never get yourself too removed from thinking in basic terms. Now to check out a line in different octaves, I will give you a transcription that resolves to the B note in the key of E at two different positions. The second half of the transcription rides the scale down from the high E string to the E on the fourth string/second fret. The last part repeats a two-note riff using the basic blue note and the tonic through three octaves.

"The next example is broken into two parts. The first passage is six notes right out of the blues scale at the fifth fret in the key of A. The second passage uses twelve notes, each half the time value of the notes used in the first passage. Notice how the second passage contains the same notes as the first one, but embellishes the first example with the bending technique and the use of relative notes.

"Repeating notes, or groups of notes, is an important technique for the lead guitarist. The repetition of a theme or passage keeps the guitarwork in one position for a longer time, rather than running out of bounds. The next example does run across a few different octaves, but notice please, that the second set of four notes is a straight repeat. This method thickens the passage so that it can stay in one range. This one is great fun and will introduce you to a truly melodic riff that has blues written all over it.

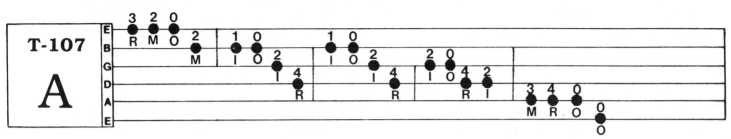

SINGING THE BLUES

"The line works over the twelve bar. When the singer starts in at the first bar, it is unusual if the melody line covers all of the available time, and this leaves space over certain bars for an instrument to put down a line. These spaces had a lot to do with the origin of jazz, because they offered a place to improvise without really interrupting the course of the song. Now as you listen to more records, you will hear all sorts of varying line structures. I don't mean just forms where the chords work themselves out in a certain way. I mean the way the melody line presents itself over the chords will vary greatly. Here are three variations of twelve-bar lines that you will hear as the records spin:

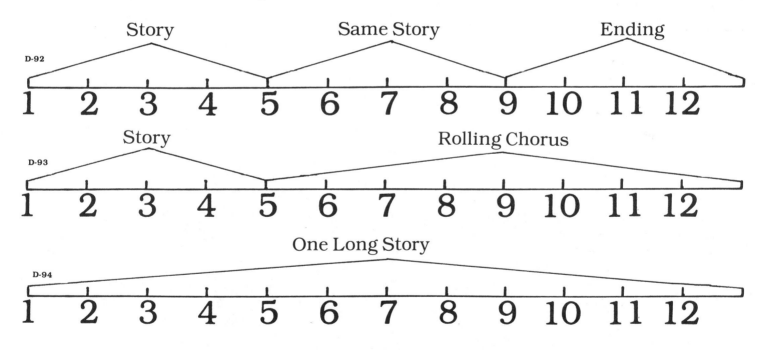

"The next example will be a trip through the twelve-bar blues from the viewpoint of a regular melody line. This example will be from the first category of the three I just listed. The idea is stated once over the first four bars, again over the next four, then finally resolved during the last four. I want you to remember that this example is typical. There is nothing special about it. It is just an example that I drew up off the top of my head. Work out the notes once, then tap your foot and try to get through it without stopping. A three-note introduction will be used that is played before the first count of the first bar. This could be considered the last count of the previous four-count twelfth bar. It is just a common lead-in. Remember, this is a melody line which is sung, so try to hum the notes as you play them and suspend the beat with the line pauses. Key of E.

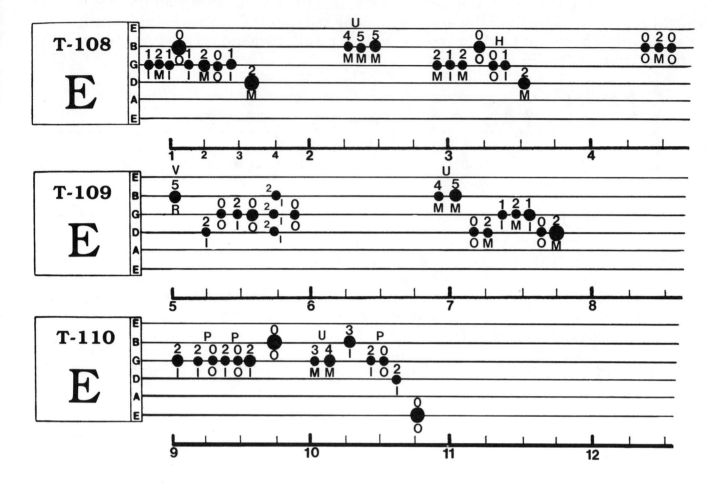

GUITAR LINE

"I know that these transcriptions aren't easy to deal with, but they are the best we have. Just try to get the feel for them and do your best to phrase the notes over the beats. With a single melody line, one of the greatest options that you have is to travel up or down into the next higher or lower octave. Get the feel for this by trying it with just a short passage. Next I want to give you a lead guitar part over the twelve bars. I kept it simple to keep the ideas clear, so you could tune in on each position. After you work it out, I'm sure that you will think of your own embellishments. Key of E."

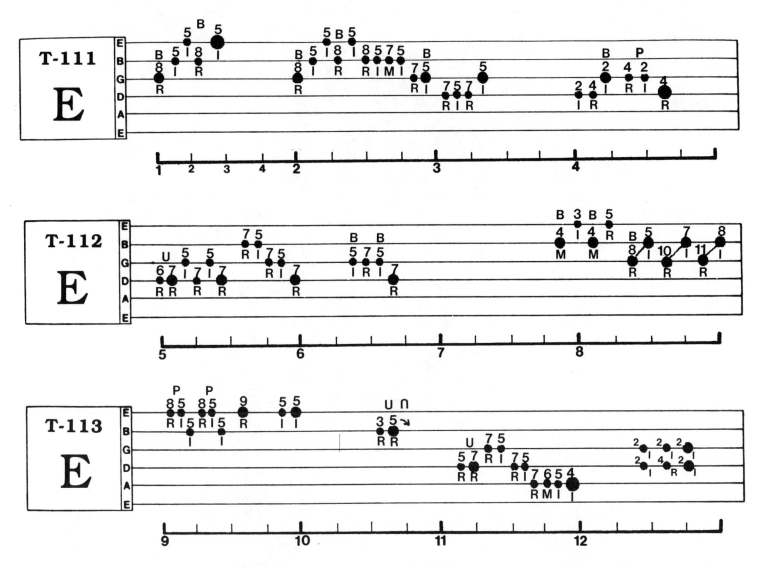

"These past two examples were designed to introduce you to the structure which you will use for most of your blues. From here on out, you will want to know specific examples of how to use the scales, chords and technique together to develop your own sound. The way I am going to tie a lot of this together is by giving you fifty short blues lead passages one after the other."

"This is what I have been waiting for, Old Man. I want those riffs. I know that you want me to understand all of the rest, but when I hear those blues riffs, I can't help myself. To me, they are what makes the blues."

"Well, Boy, I feel you've earned your keep. So I won't make you wait any longer."

16. Fifty Blues Moves

ubbles on top of the beer. That's what blues riffs are like, Boy. First off, you have to go through all of the trouble to brew the beer, bottle it, transport it, chill it and pour it into a glass. After you have a full glass, these little bubbles appear out of the bulk volume of liquid and come to the top where they pop, fizz, manifest themselves in a million different little ways for a brief moment — and then go away. Now that you are tempered, I feel you are ready for a few of the trade secrets.''

The afternoon sun poured light onto the kitchen table as the old man opened a can of cold beer. ''Things get clearer with use, Boy. This is a rule I want you to find out first hand. Books and papers are only a means to an end. Thing is, without those examples that the paper provides, you end up playing the same thing over and over. Get intense with both polar regions. Study hard, play hard.''

The boy hung on every word the old man said as he tuned his guitar in anticipation of the promised blues riffs. ''Now I'm going to give you a string of bits and pieces that will eventually form a general body of knowledge that you can apply to practically any type of blues guitarwork. Some of the moves will set you up in a unique pattern and you will be expected to work out your own riffs from this single position. Others will be precise individual riffs to be played exactly as transcribed, and are laden with technique symbols and different size dots to indicate the duration of the notes. Some will seem to present ideas that you already know, but, as I told you before, *never underestimate the familiar.* The best and the worst music all come from the same six strings. The best you can do is lock the woodshed door, run it down until you have callouses, then spring it on the world all at once. Lock everything else out right now, Boy. We're going into it.

''I will present you with the moves one at a time. Each will be clearly numbered in sequence and identified by key in the box to the left of the transcription. Some, but not all, will name the basic fret that is used in this same box. A few of the transcriptions will be divided into several sections by full bar lines. Mini-bars are used in many of the transcriptions just to clarify the deal. They are not necessarily meant to indicate a pause, but in cases such as triplets, you will be expected to phrase accordingly. Double line bars are used to set off introduction chords that set you up for the move, but are not really part of the passage itself.

Move 1

"We will kick it off along the root note fret in the key of A at the fifth fret. This first move is broken into seven different bars, each of which sheds a little light on the most basic position for lead guitar. Get ready to put the index across the two thin strings, and please take the time to check out the difference between each short passage. Don't say I never took the time to show you the little things.

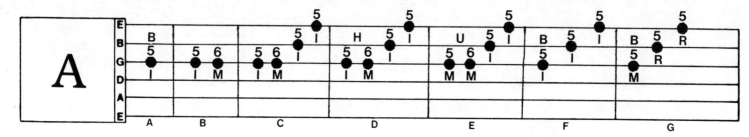

Move 2

"This one starts off with the D bar from Move 1 and then rolls right down the notes over the root note fret. Watch for chromatic step hammers because they take a second to figure out — especially the double hammer on the fifth string. Work with it dry, then try to make your music.

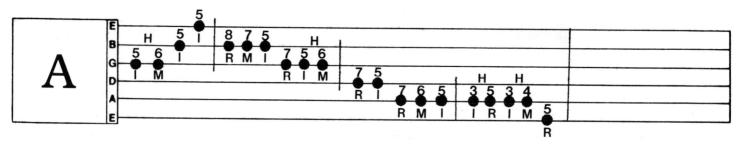

Move 3

"This guy breaks through the usual barriers as it walks the board vertically down to the open strings. Starting on the twelfth fret octave mark in the key of E, we use the first and third string in various configurations to walk it down in triplets. Watch your fingering and hammer on the first note of the last triplet at the open strings.

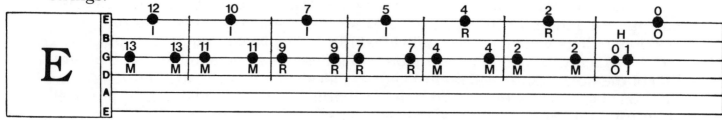

Move 4

"Slide up the first note with the middle finger, then work your way up to bend that blue note on the first string at the eighth fret. The very last note makes the riff, so slide it up to sound that tonic A note with confidence. B. B. King uses this slide a lot to get at that all-important key note from the bottom.

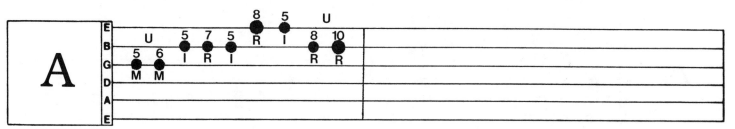

Move 5

"This move shows you a two-chord sequence in three positions: the root note fret for the keys of A, D and E. The first chord is the major on the top three strings, the second one is the seventh for the tonic. After you've got it, try sliding the second chord up to its position four frets above the root note fret.

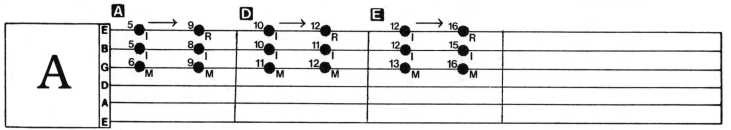

Move 6

"This is a double-note study using the index to hold down two strings. The way to make it happen is to practice letting the strings ring before you hammer. Bring the hammer finger down hard, Boy!

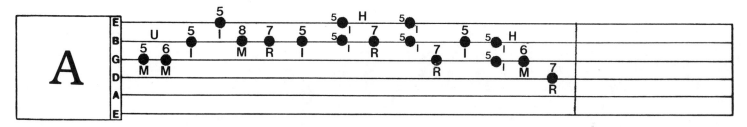

Move 7

"The double bend on the first and third notes are the big ones! Make them roll until you can play them as one. There is an unusual slide on the third string that goes over the root note fifth fret. Hold the last note.

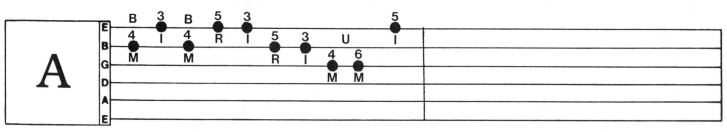

Move 8

"This has always been one of my favorites. Here is what real blues guitar is all about! Play each note distinctly as you walk down. The clincher is the last note — slide it down from the fifth fret with the index and let it ring. This special note is the star from the *symbols to understand* and is the third from the major chord.

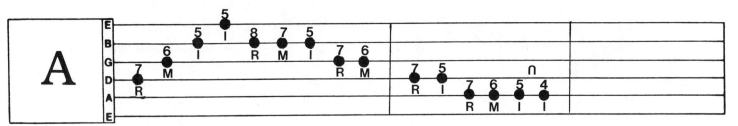

Move 9

"This is real delta stuff! First I show you the base seventh chord in E. You take the notes from this chord on the second and third strings and play only them, sliding them up from under. Play the E string open during the repeat. Walk it down starting with that bend/pull, then walk it up through two octaves starting with the low string open.

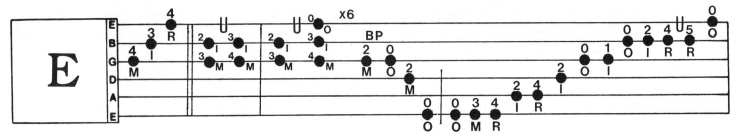

Move 10

"Watch for the first bend in this one because the first note after the bend is three frets above the root note fret. Also watch for the double pull which takes considerable practice before mastering. Read carefully.

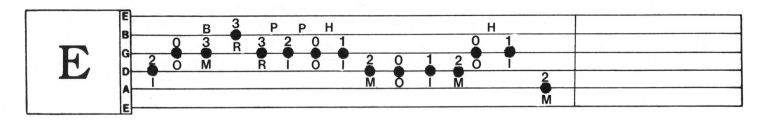

Move 11

"This move uses the same notes as the previous move, but the index finds itself up on the third fret after the 3-4 slide on the third string. The double pull is still there for you to practice. I told you it takes awhile to get it down!

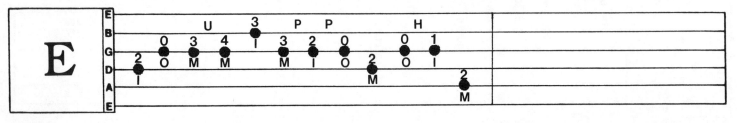

Move 12

"Repetition is the key to this move. The first bar takes you through, the second repeats two notes, and the third plays a repeated note. This might not seem like an earth-shaking discovery, but repeating can keep you from falling into just running the scales when you should be building up a classy lick.

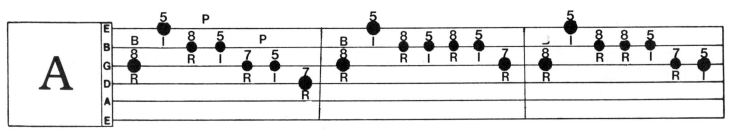

Move 13

"Bend the first note, then get ready to take it up to the eighth fret with the index. I'm trying to show you the whole thing in pieces, Boy, so just trust me and do it.

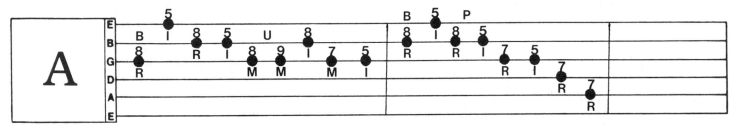

Move 14

"Move over Chuck and Elmore, because the Boy knows your riffs. The index double string does the talking. The notes that follow the repeating double-note sequence should be studied closely, especially the last one that has the triple bend with the index finger. You don't have to bend it a half-step. A little bit with feeling will do!

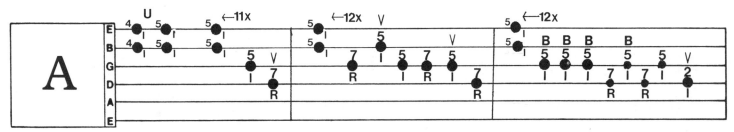

Move 15

"Here are three sister riffs that work along the fifth fret. The first one belongs to the index as it works the fret one string after the other. Make sure to bend the first note. The second brings down the hammer as does the third after going back to the tonic twice.

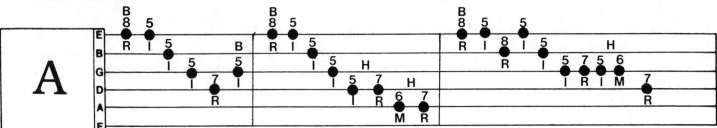

Move 16

"I'm going to show you the same cards in two decks. The first hand plays out on the third and fourth string, complete with double pull. The second one is an octave higher on the two thin strings, so plant your index on the third fret and work above with others.

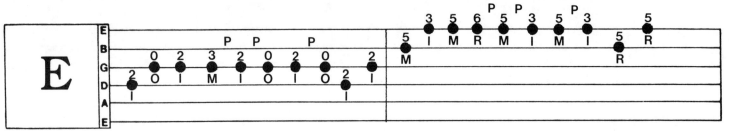

Move 17

"Start off with a slide, then center the index at the eighth fret. Small dot double triplets bring it home to the root note fret to finish it up.

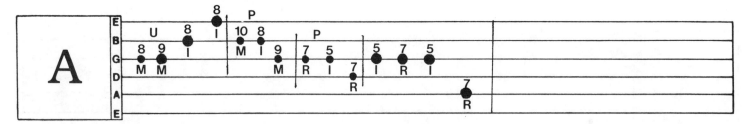

Move 18

"This move uses relative notes above the root note fret. Watch for that six to appear on the third string, and for the double note ending.

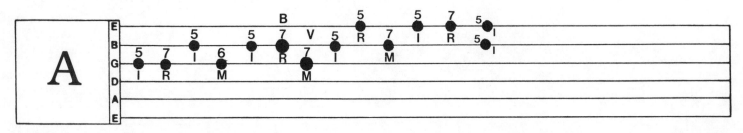

Move 19

"You remember the suspended chord deal? It uses the fourth of the major scale on top of the major triad. Here I show you how to use the suspended note as a hammer on in three positions: A, D and E. The last three bars lay on an additional sixth. Sounds pretty, doesn't it? Sure is movable, too.

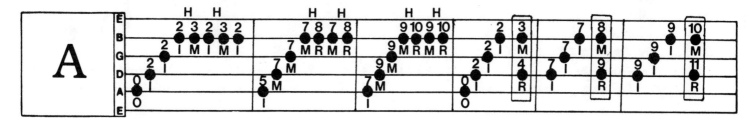

Move 20

"Here is a look at the open string position for the blues scale in A. Notice how the repeated hammer is on the third string rather than the fourth string for E. Watch your technique symbols. The last bar shows you the relative scale along the second fret and on the three low strings. Work with it.

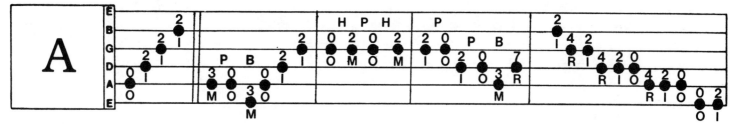

Move 21

"Certain chords can be easily moved around and the major seventh is one of them. I spell it out for you in the first bar. Played with the ring and middle on the seventh fret, the chord is a D major seventh, but the first bar shows you the slide that works for the A centered fifth fret. Watch that double note slide. The last bar shows you the game for the E centered twelfth fret.

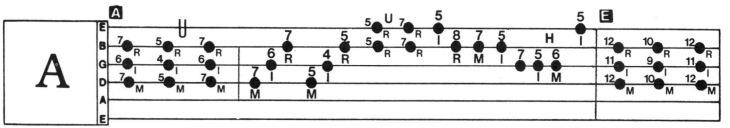

Move 22

"This move is typical of what a clarinet or sax would play as a filler for a classic blues. Very melodic use of the major scale is in full evidence. The slide up after the mini-bar shows you another position above the major chord. End on that high tonic note, second string.

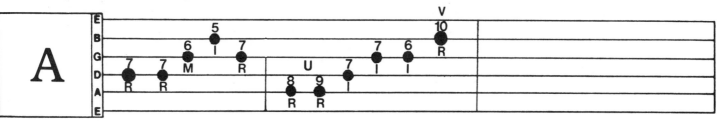

Move 23

"Start off with sliding up a seventh chord position to the A position on the fifth fret. After you climb up 3, 4, 5 on the fifth string, situate your fingers into a fixed chord, then play across the fret with a broken chord technique.

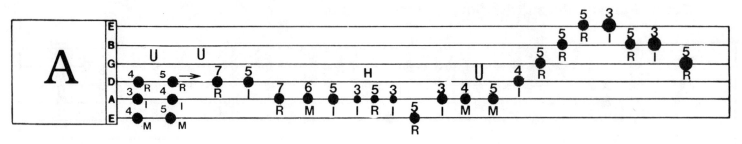

Move 24

"Focus on the open string position in E. Be forceful with the repeated hammer on the fourth string. Then pull your way down to the blue note on fatty. The same deal on the upper strings ending with that high tonic on the second string.

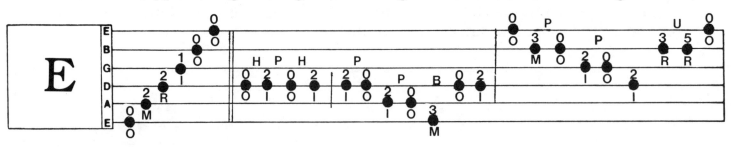

Move 25

"After you play an E major chord at the bottom, and run the blues scale over the open strings, try this mellow relative climb-up through the octaves. It starts on the sixth string open and goes up to the first string. A blue note is used as a filler.

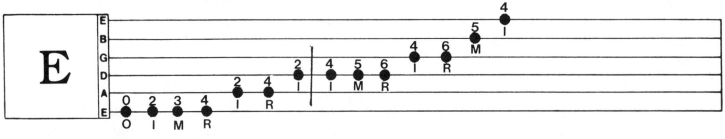

Move 26

"This move employs the common filler note between the fourth and fifth, known as the diamond from *symbols to understand*. I'm showing you three different ways, in three different octaves. It's just a filler, Boy.

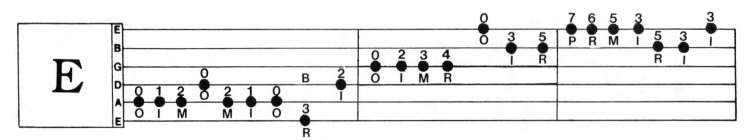

Move 27

"First center the index, middle and ring in the major position shown in the first bar. The second bar shows notes that can be played with the pinky and then we move onto chords that the pinky can make by coming down on to the chord. The last bar plays a nice riff that has a jazz feel to it.

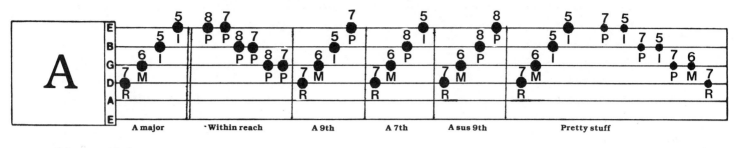

Move 28

"This is the first of a series of resolutions. Make your regular E chord at the bottom then play the third and fifth string and move them up one fret at a time. The final B seventh chord resolves the move.

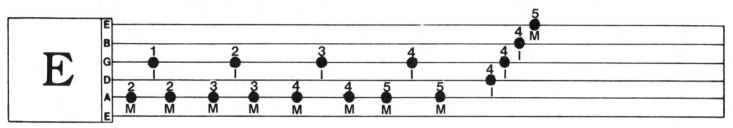

Move 29

"The first bar shows an easy way to reach a B seventh chord from the bottom. This is a great resolution for use with the E and A chord in their basic position. The second bar shows you a resolution using the standard A chord moved up two frets into the B major chord position.

Move 30

"Okay, the first bar takes the A seventh position at the bottom and through two steps, raises it to a B seventh chord. The second bar does the same thing with the three upper strings from the E bar chord on the fifth, sixth and seventh frets. The final chord shown is a B seventh position which works four frets above the root note fret.

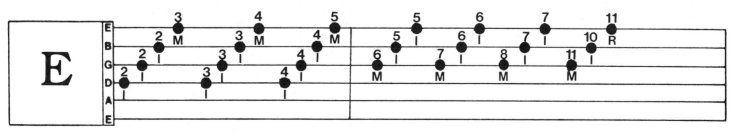

Move 31

"This guy is actually a lead-in to resolution. Walk it down chromatically, making sure that you play the hammers from the example in the first bar. The second bar plays the same dude in a lower octave.

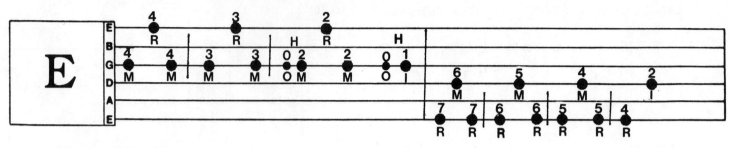

Move 32

"It goes on, Boy. The first bar walks down the whole three-string position of the familiar seventh position on the top three strings. The second bar walks down the same path, only this time, we leave the high string open.

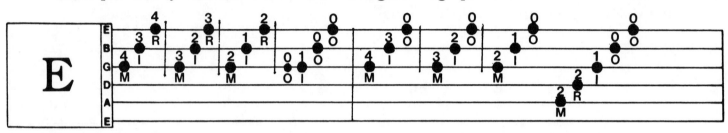

Move 33

"Here is a resolution for the key of A. The first bar shows you a walk down using the first and third strings which ends on the major chord, fifth fret. The second bar is the same riff, but an octave lower.

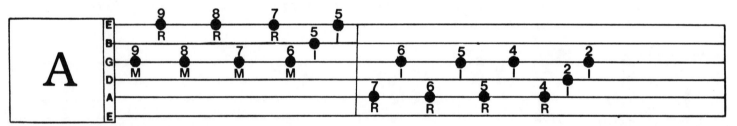

Move 34

"The first bar is my favorite resolution in E. It combines some of the approaches that we have been studying. The final bar pushes a three-string seventh chord position up to the B position at the seventh fret.

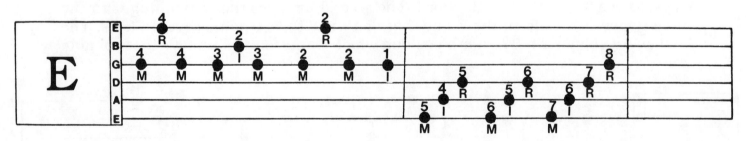

Move 35

"Did I ever tell you that the relative scale is the same as the major with the fourth and the seventh omitted? It's true. You can call it a new scale if you want, but if you add the fourth to the relative scale, you have a very melodic vehicle. Think in terms of using the relative scale pattern with the addition of a single note. This added note is a D note for the relative scale in the key of A and has a small star above it in the following transcription.

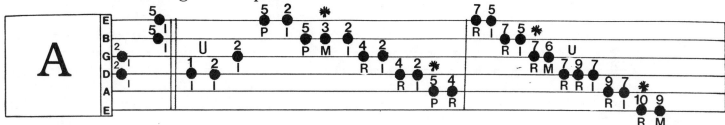

Move 36

"Try swinging the first two pairs of notes, slightly bending them to get extra texture. Bend that high note and then walk it down until you play the third, fourth and fifth strings all with the middle finger. These final notes should be played one string at a time, moving the middle to each string.

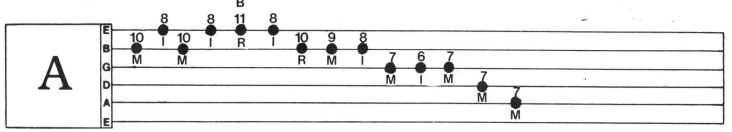

Move 37

"Time to try octaves, Boy. Open with a rhythm riff in the key of E. Keeping the index and ring at a fixed distance and smooth sliding are the keys to successful execution.

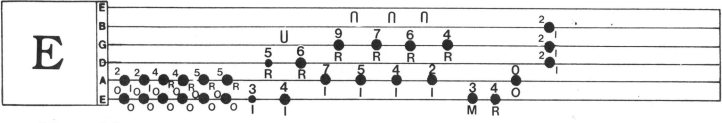

Move 38

"This one should be played in a single roll. The double bends with the index and the chromatic rolls can make it come alive if you try hard enough. I threw in a seventh bar chord at the end.

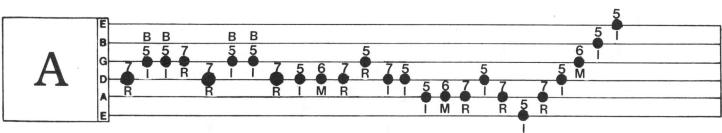

Move 39

"This one takes a sense of phrasing. The first two notes move a slow tonic down to the flatted seventh. Then you roll over the same chromatic run, both up and down, before you end up on the same note that you started on.

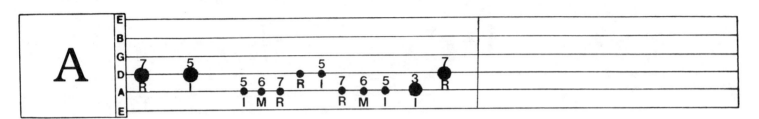

Move 40

"Subtle bending is the secret of this one. Like I said, there is no law that says you have to bend a note a half-step if you set out to bend. You can bend it just a touch and nobody is going to handcuff you. Try it on all four bends that you see here.

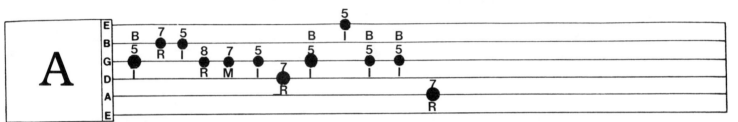

Move 41

"Bend and pull with a fierce fury, Boy. Attack your guitar. Wear it out and I'll give you two more! Bend, pull, slide up and roll above the root note fret on the thin strings. Then listen to the records and you will find the same.

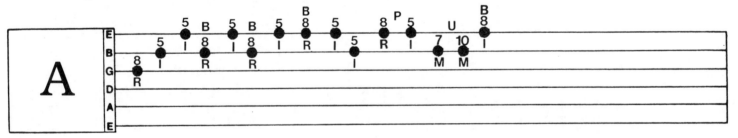

Move 42

"The first three notes are a bend and hold that don't use the index. Check out the three sets of four that work down the strings. See how fast you can play them, then remember them for later use with any pattern.

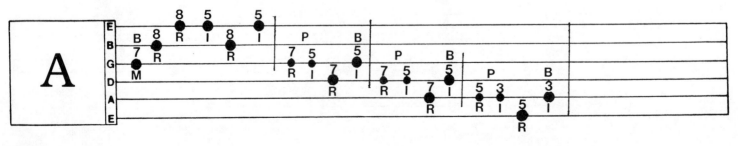

Move 43

"This transcription only paints a picture for what should be a fluid chord trick. This is a way to go from the first to the fourth chord without moving your hand too much. Pinky trick is shown first, then ring slap over. Once you bar, the slap goes to the pinky. The T on the low E string fingering means thumb. Jimi did, you should try, too.

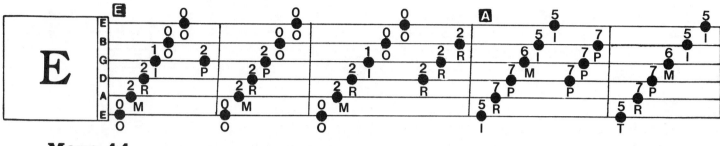

Move 44

"Chromatic time. Check out the weirdo on the fifth string. You will see that anything is really playable after a while. You just have to think of it. Don't forget the double triplet, with index adjustment, on the third string.

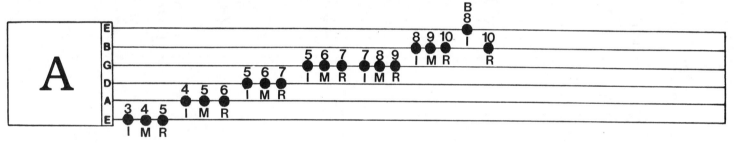

Move 45

"Double note possibilities are explored here. The transcription is busy, but it does work if you do. Three sets of two, with the middle one altered is the way it goes.

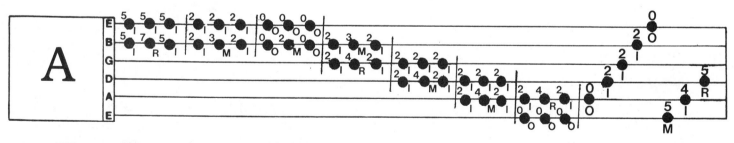

Move 46

"I put this one in to give you an idea of how the major scale can work out. You will find minor notes mixed in with the major scale degrees as you go. Sets of four all the way up.

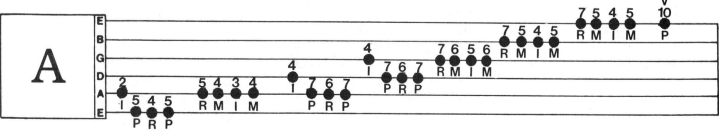

Move 47

"By now you know that the basic 'index across the root note fret on the two thin strings' produces the first and the fifth of the scale. Now I'm going to show you the places where this deal appears on the E blues board. The guitar will open up to you, Boy, if you jump in.

Move 48

"We're back to that repeat double note opening. The double notes come after that, so move them down in sets. Then the game goes back to double note play on the second and third string, followed by relative leadwork.

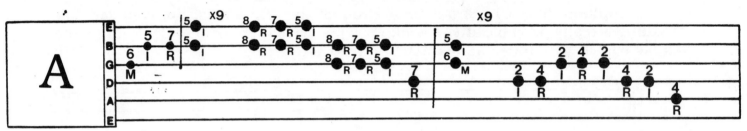

Move 49

"Out of breath, Boy? Don't give up yet! Herein lies the difference between the blues and the relative scale. First I show you a useful box in the E blues, then the same box in the relative.

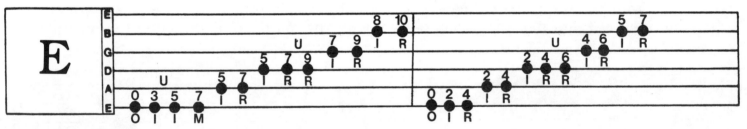

Move 50

"The last one is short but sweet! It works out on only the second string and shows you the difference between a whole-step bend and a half-step bend. After you think you know the move, try it out on the high E string in the same position."

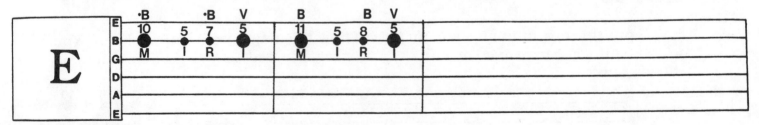

The boy set his guitar against the kitchen table and drew in a long breath. The old man sat back on the kitchen bench and strummed a single E chord, letting the strings' action decay until the wooden box no longer produced sound.

"You are as me, Boy. We stand alone at the base of the mountain."

17. Crossed, Open, Slide

Way back when, down on the Mississippi plantations, the field workers used to take a single strand of wire that held the straw around an old broom handle and stretch it between two nails driven into the wooden wall of a shack. A rock was forced under the wire to increase the tension of the wire and gave the would-be musician something he could use to change the pitch of the string. Just imagine the sound that one string made — a single whining, steely cry sustained by the wallboard! It was around this time that the use of the string slide, a piece of hard material such as glass or metal worn or held by the fingers of the left hand, caught on widely throughout the delta region.'' The old man took a clear glass slide and placed it on the kitchen table for the boy to examine.

''Blues guitarists use all sorts of things for slides, such as knife blades, metal tubes worn over the fingers, wide finger rings, or inch-long sections of cut bottlenecks worn on the pinky. The effect is much the same no matter what is used. The string vibrates in a fundamental wavelength between the point where the slide touches the string and the fixed bridge at the bottom of the guitar. Sliding allows you to approach the guitar as a fretless instrument because, unlike fretting which fixes the string to intervals of a half-step, the slide sweeps along the surface of the linear string. This results in a constantly increasing, or decreasing pitch as the slide moves along the strings' length. Ideally, the slide never brings the string down onto the fret but rides like a bicycle on a high wire in a circus act.

''What are the implications here, Boy? First off, in order to produce a desired note, you have to bring the slide to an *exact point* on the string directly over the fret. To fret a string, you bring the steel strand down with the finger onto the wood of the board anywhere between two given frets. The slide does not offer the force against the string that fretting does, but relies on common string tension to keep the slide against the string. Although using a slide requires you to be more accurate, you are also afforded certain freedoms. The pitch of a sounded note is constantly affected by the slide's touch. You are free to make the smallest up or down adjustment to get exactly the note that you want. You can make a fretted note increase in pitch by slightly bending the string across the board. However, there is nothing you can do, short of retuning, to make that fretted note *lower* in pitch if you are tuned sharp.

"Just as any movement of the finger changes the character of the fretted note, the movement of the slide on the string determines the sound quality of a note produced. You can slowly slide up and bring the correct note in with a steady hand, sounding a smooth, unvarying note. You can also vibrate the slide on the string to create an uneasy, shaky note like the hyperactive slashing sound you hear on Elmore James' records. Try arriving at your destination note from a higher pitch by sliding down from above or overshoot your mark and then come back. I'm telling you, it isn't as easy as it might first seem.

"Consider how many strings you want to play with the slide. There are guys I know who use only the top string in their style, but the top two or three strings played together are the most commonly used strings for the slide guitarist. You are stuck with a straight bar, so position your slide level with the board and parallel to the direction of the frets. Sliding is the sort of thing you shouldn't talk too much about. You have to see if you've got the knack by putting the slide on the strings. It's best to mute the strings with the first or second finger behind the slide. This cuts down the strings' vibration on the other side of the slide going towards the nut, and reduces extraneous sliding sounds. Another way of cutting back on extraneous sound is by placing the slide over only the strings that you want to use starting from the thin strings down. Of course, when the guitar is tuned to an open chord you can put the slide across all six and move it around to different tonic centers which take their positions over the frets. The fifth fret is the A center, seventh is B, eighth is C, three is G, ten is D, nine is C, twelve is E, and the first is F. For the key of E our centers are the open string, fifth fret, seventh fret, and a second tonic center on twelve double dot. For the key of A it is the fifth fret, the tenth fret, and the twelfth or open string position. How am I doing, Boy?

"Any note you fret can also be played with the slide. If you use the slide on the lower strings exculsively, you might want to tilt the slide a bit so you don't drag on the thinner strings unnecessarily. That slide sure sounds dirty on those low wound strings, just how I like it.

"The right hand can be used to mute specific strings by placing the fingertips on your chosen string down by the bridge. Try using the palm of the hand between the little finger and the wrist for silencing a string that you want to stop ringing. Speaking of the right hand, try picking alternate strings, like the first and the third, skipping over the second with the old flatpick. Ouch, that's for 'pinching' two strings at once and then sliding the two strings simultaneously.

"Now, don't think that because you put a piece of glass or metal on your finger that the scale patterns have changed. Everything remains the same in that department except that you have to play *over* rather than *between* frets. Here is a common box for A and E that you can use to get acquainted with the slide. The transcription shows ascending, descending and double notes. Fine tune your senses, Boy, and bring those notes in.

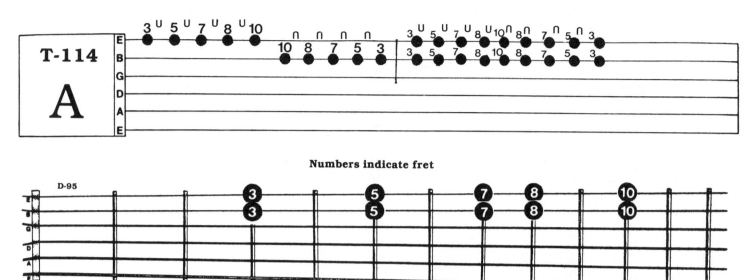

Numbers indicate fret

"If you work with the slide for one evening, it will come clear to you which systems you will have to fool with in order to get good riffs. You are always working across one fret whenever you are playing more than one note. As far as traveling up and down the direction of the strings, well, you see that slide is always on that string unless you take it off for dipping. So, if you have an interval of say three frets and you don't need the intermediate chromatic degrees, well, you start to see that muting is a big part of the picture for some styles. For starters, I would choose one or two riffs that you know from regular fretting and work just with them for an evening rather than getting in over your head. It will dawn on you later if you think about it directly for now.

"Slide forces you to look at the little things because the movement of the slide has a critical tolerance factor that is very steep indeed. I mean the *slightest* movement, Boy. If you are a bit off, you have a sour note. We know the blues allows for sour notes, but what I'm talking about is lemon sour! No good! Concentrate on a sparse style at first, one where you bring in a few sweet notes to just the right pitch.

OPEN TUNING

"Like the water runs down the hill, the open strings of the guitar invited the old blues players to tune their guitars to play a major chord by just strumming the strings open. This involves tuning the strings up or down from their standard tuning pitches to accomodate scale degrees which occur in the desired chord. There are many ways in which you can tune your wonderful instrument, Boy. Here is a limited list. Altered strings are underlined.

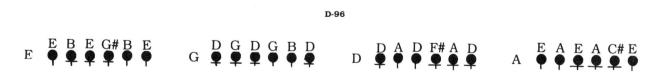

"Open tuning can turn the six strings of the guitar into a mini-orchestra. The open string tuning of a stringed instrument goes way back in history — thousands of years! Playing in open tuning without fretting can be an inspirational experience. This is why some blues guys have freewheeling fingerpicking styles all figured out. It's just easy to do.

"So what are the implications of tuning open, Boy? Well, for one thing, the patterns of the blues and relative patterns are going to be different. I didn't say gone. I didn't say impossible. I said *different*. For instance, tune your guitar to an E chord and then try these fun guys for rocking.

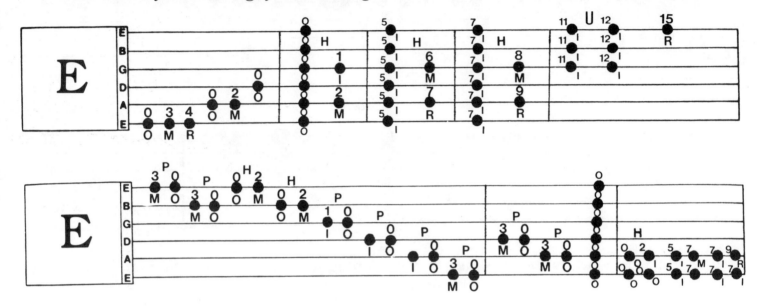

"The third and fourth bars give you a nifty overlaying pattern that looks like the regular E seventh chord until you bring it down on the open strings. We've got just the open strings. We've got lead patterns from the various scales. We have lay-over patterns that we hammer on. We've got movable major chords by just bringing down a finger on a fret. We've got the movable rhythm riff with just two fingers.

"It was the blues that caused the successful marriage of slide guitar to open tuning. Just listen to the old records and it won't be long until you hear it happen. To find the fourth and the fifth major chords above any tonic note center, just go up five and seven frets.

CROSSED

"The word 'crossed' has been used to describe open tuning. But it is usually a term which refers to playing a harmonica in a different key from its designated tonic key. Here is the low-down. If you want to play the blues with a harp in the key of E, you buy a harp stamped 'A.' You count up five frets from the key you want to play in and buy the harp stamped with that tonic key. The reason for this is the E seventh scale, that is the seven-note E major scale with a flatted seventh, is the same as the major scale in the key of A. I usually just keep a few of them around stamped with D and A so that I can play my blues. If somebody says they can play one, I say 'Go ahead and do it'."

18. You Heard It, You Play It.

"Tape is a miracle, I'll tell you that right now, Boy." The old man stood up from the kitchen table and headed for the downstairs door. "Come on, Boy. There are a few tape recorders down in the basement I want to set up so I can drive home a point to your blue mind."

Once again they walked down the basement stairs to the room where the old man had shown the boy the blues record archive. "It's funny how it works out, Boy," the old man said as he kicked open the door.

"How's that, Old Man?"

"Well, sometimes you don't really need help driving the car. You only need help with directions to know which road to go down. Seems to me this might apply to you at this time, Boy. You walk up to me on the tracks and ask me to teach you blues guitar. So, I tell you all about how to play blues guitar. Your cherry red '56 Chevy is running right now, but do you have the map? I gave you fifty bubbles. That's nothing compared to what's going on in that bottle of champagne. So, how are you going to get a hundred more? How are you going to teach yourself, Boy? Well, listen to me now because what I am about to say I really believe in my heart is true.

"You can teach yourself any style of blues, rock or popular guitar directly from tape recordings of the best artists in the field of your choice. Think of it, Boy. I'm not talking about just giving a listen to a few riffs. There are thousands of recordings in the fields of jazz, blues, rock, soul and popular. And you can learn any riff on any of the records that you hear."

"I don't know, Old Man. I'm not that good at picking things off the record. Everything seems to move too fast for me. I can figure out what key the song is in, but everything after that is a blur. When I stop the record, I forget what I'm supposed to copy."

"That's alright, Boy. You just need a few directions." The old man rushed

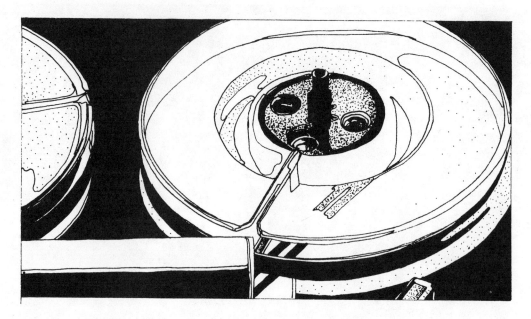

around the room plugging in wires to a reel-to-reel tape recorder, hooking it to the back of a stereo amplifier. "Now let's just say that there is a great guitar break on a record that you hear and you want to figure it out. Let me give you the sequence to do just that.

"First of all, the guitar break that you are interested in was played on a six string guitar just like yours. This sounds elementary, but it is important to realize that this is an actual fact. His guitar is like yours. Now, what happened the day the recording was made? Well, the guitarist played his guitar and, depending on if it was an electric or acoustic, either shook the air in the recording studio with the wooden body of the guitar, or with the speakers of an amplifier. So we have this disturbed air — soundwaves — headed in the direction of a sensitive microphone. The waves reach the mike and physically move a sensitive mechanism which translates the movement of the air into tiny electrical impulses which are run down the mike chord to a recording amplifier whose output is connected to a recording head. This recording head is the heart of any tape recording machine and is actually a horseshoe shaped electromagnet with a narrow gap between its two pole pieces. The more narrow the gap, the greater the fidelity.

"The magnetic tape which we run over the head and keep on reserve spools is very long and thin. It's made of plastic and is coated on one side with a magnetic compound. During the recording process, the tape is pulled evenly over the head and variations in the magnetic field of the horseshoe magnet produces an almost exact image in the magnetization of the coating on the tape. Now, the tape has the message from the mike stored or 'recorded' on it. During playback, the opposite thing takes place. The tape acts as the master, setting up slight electrical charges in the playback head, which in turn, runs down the wire to the amp and then to the speakers in the room. What I'm getting at is this: the artist plays a note on the guitar and it is a 440 A. It gets recorded on all of this strange modern day stuff and then is played back at exactly a 440 A. The same note that the guitarist played is now playing out into this room. In this way we can summon up any recording that we want and make it dance right here, right now!

"A lot of people will tell you that it's no good to copy records because it's 'not original.' They can't get themselves past that word 'copy.' I might agree with them if the guitarist doing the copying was a professional who went out and played another artist's work in order to make money with the copy of the material. That is not what I'm advising you. There are so many albums that there is an ocean of perfected style out in the record bins. Why shouldn't the student quickly advance his style by checking out what the possibilities are? The people that made those records have gone before you in the blues heritage and I think it's important for you to see what they realized. The scales are dry cardboard cutouts. If I lock you in a room with the scales, you get good at climbing scales. But by analyzing finished recordings, you can push your style ahead faster than any other means I know of. Let yourself be influenced. In a way, it is impossible to copy someone else because they're not you! Besides, why do you think early Clapton records sound so much like Albert King? Why did young Robert Johnson sit at the feet of Son House? What did Keith and Mick do with all of those records that they ordered from Chess Records? You're next, Boy.

"Now, let's say that you have a recording you want to figure out. It doesn't have to be a lead guitar riff. It can be anything that you hear on a record. I want to show you how this can be done so you can do it on your own." The old man produced an old record of traditional American songs. "First, I will locate what we want to know on the record and just play it a few times."

The old man put the tone arm of the turntable down on the record and the beginning of the *National Anthem* blared out of the speakers in the corner of the room. "Now you've heard it, Boy, now you play it," the old man said as he lifted the tone arm off the record.

"First off, we have to make a tape recording, so we run auxilary wires to the back of our reel-to-reel and record our passage. There are three common speeds on the reel-to-reel and only one speed on the cassette deck. If you can possibly get an old reel-to-reel, that is the ideal situation. The cheapest cassette player that makes noise will suffice if you want it to bad enough. I will now record the beginning of the *National Anthem* on the reel-to-reel, at the middle speed which uses 3-3/4 inches of tape per second.

"Now, turn the record player off, wind the tape to zero, tune the guitar to concert pitch, set the tape counter to zero, and play the tape." The beginning of the anthem started to play, but the old man cut it short with the pause button. He rewound it to the zero mark and played the beginning again and again. "You are not interested in entertainment here, Boy. All you want to hear are those notes! I mean THOSE NOTES! Just those notes that are sung for the words 'Oh say can you'."

The old man rewound the tape to the zero mark for the fifth time. "Now, listen to this, Boy. I am going to slow the tape down to the lower speed from the middle speed. This reduces the speed of the tape over the head to 1-7/8 inches of tape per second — or half of that of the middle speed. This will be half as fast, and one octave below what you just heard five times."

The old man played the tape and the words to the anthem came out of the speaker in a long, low drawl. "Now I'm going in on it, Boy." Intensity flashed in the old man's eyes as he sat down in front of the tape deck with his guitar. "I'm at zero now, at slow speed, and I'm going to play only the first note."

Just the first note played out of the speakers. The old man quickly hit the pause. He repeated the process again and again, playing only the first note. "Now that note is planted in your mind deep enough, Boy. You know that the note is one of the twelve — which is it?"

The boy started to play the chromatic scale until he came upon the familiar note. The boy looked up and smiled.

"I happen to know that the sequence for the opening notes of the anthem are two descending quarter notes for the word 'oh' and a whole note each for 'say can you' played in ascending order." The boy played the notes after hunting for a few seconds.

"Now I'll put the recorder back to normal speed, que it up to zero and watch you play the first five notes. Ready?"

The boy nodded with his finger already holding the first note, his face in deep concentration. The old man pressed the 'play' button and the boy played the first five notes with the recording. The old man let the tape spin on past the beginning. "You know *how to use* the tape recorder, but you have to teach yourself to *teach yourself.* You have to go through the struggle of doing it yourself the first time. From there on in you will have your balloon airborne. What I will do now is leave you with this cassette player for an hour. Here is a cassette tape which has a very slow blues lead on it in the key of A. I want you to listen to the whole song once, then go back to the beginning. Play the tape up to the start of the guitar break. Stop the machine, set the counter to zero, and proceed. The tempo is slow and the guitar plays single notes out of A. USE THE BUTTONS. USE THE BUTTONS. USE THE BUTTONS on this silly little machine with the spool of tape hidden in it. You are the hunter. You will find just that second of tape where the guitar break begins. Then, using the 'rewind' button, PIN IT DOWN. Shut the recorder off, pick up your guitar and start hunting for your game to work out along the root note fifth fret. If it's not there, go down to the relative and hunt around. Remember, HIS GUITAR IS JUST LIKE YOURS AND HE HAD TO PLAY IT SOMEHOW. BRING IT OUT INTO THE LIGHT OF DAY. FREE THE BLUES FROM THAT TAPE AND PLAY THEM OUT INTO THIS ROOM ON YOUR GUITAR. See you in an hour, Boy."

The old man walked slowly up the stairs as the boy turned the cassette player on.

19. Tonight is Every Night

After an hour's passing, the old man tiptoed down the wooden stairs to the door at the bottom of the stairwell. Through the door he could hear the boy playing lead guitar note-for-note over the recording. Kicking the door open, the old man made his entrance.

"Worked out on the fifth fret just like I said, didn't it, Boy? I know, because I figured it out myself. The recorder is great for finding out the pitch of a note. But sometimes you might have a problem finding the box that the artist actually used for his leadwork. It gets to be like a jigsaw puzzle. But you can figure it out if you listen closely enough. Don't forget — you have higher and lower octaves, and also different positions in the same octave. At any rate, you'll find seventy percent of blues and rock leads straight along the root note fret."

The boy looked up to the old man to see that he'd changed his dress to work boots and a new denim jacket. The boy was full of energy and wanted to tell the old man of his new discoveries, but held off until he could understand the change he felt was taking place. The old man looked younger as he hurried around the room putting things away. The boy could sense a direct, urgent energy in the old man's actions, as if he was ready to step out.

"Grab your guitar, Boy. We're moving down to the rails. Bring the game into a wider scope and forget your fingertips for awhile. You have done well, and now that you can use the recorder to advance yourself, you have your work cut out. COME ON BOY, tie your shoes and let's get out of here."

The boy didn't ask any questions. He stood up and readied himself as the old man led the way up the stairs into the kitchen. "I've got the flask of brandy, Boy, so take whatever guitar you want. Grab a handful of picks, harps, strings and things and follow me down."

The old man walked through the rooms of the house making one final check. Holding the kitchen door for the boy, he turned out the lights and stepped out onto the porch.

"Do you live here, Old Man?" the boy asked.

"Not really," the old man said, adjusting the leather day pack over his shoulder and sliding the key under the door mat. "There are other houses, Boy."

The boy asked no more, but walked with the old man through the night air down to the tracks. The rails made a large sweeping curve into the woods where the old man and the boy stepped up onto the bed of cinders.

"You have to be careful out on the tracks, Boy. You have to look up and down at the same time." The boy looked twice at the old man, realizing that it was the first time in days that the old man had talked about anything other than music.

The old man walked off to the side of the tracks and picked up an old newspaper that was lying by the wayside. "Ready to jump the train, Boy? It will be here in a minute or two."

The boy heard nothing, but knew that he soon would. "I don't know, Old Man. I just don't know."

The old man took a pack of matches out of his pocket and proceeded to light the newspaper on fire. "Come on, Boy. Run with me on this road by the tracks. Run for your life. Run for the blues. Run for this night."

With guitars in hand, the two bluesmen took off running down the railroad utility road. The boy was too out of breath to stop to ask any questions as the old man stopped and crawled under a group of low lying bushes on the outside curve of the tracks.

"Come on, Boy. Get under here and hide." The train blasted its whistle as the light from the engine pierced through the night. "She's rolling right this second, Boy, and she's long. The engineer slows it down when he sees the fire to make sure he's going onto safe tracks." The engine passed by with its long line of cars in tow when the old man jumped out of the bushes commanding the boy to follow.

"She's slow enough now, Boy, and getting slower. Let's jump on. I'm making your mind up for you, Boy. After ten cars, we jump. Don't think, DO."

Everything happened in a blur. The next thing he knew, the boy was rolling on the boards of a boxcar floor.

"I think I scratched my guitar a little bit, Old Man," the boy remarked, swaying back and forth with the movement of the train.

"Well then, Boy, have a sip of this brandy and carve the date next to the scratch." The old man laughed and laughed.

"At least I didn't have to watch you howl at the train like a coyote this time, Old Man."

The old man pulled a small portable cassette player out of his bag and slid it across the wooden planks to the boy. "There's your machine, Boy. On the tape inside it you will find twenty great blues standards. Figure out the guitarwork on these songs note-for-note. Build the riffs you find into your vocabulary and you will have your wings. Now don't forget to look for those relative riffs to work out three frets below the root note fret. Watch for those *symbols to understand,* because they are guaranteed to pop up right in the middle of a blues scale lick. Practice barring your rhythm riff, centering it on the sixth or fifth strings. Practice your chromatic fingering exercises along with your blues, relative and major scale fingerings. Throw your techniques and pinky hammer-ons into the pot, stir in some phrasing and a little bit of soul — and you've got blues soup.

"Concerning that recorder, make sure that you get the knack of queueing it up to zero with the rewind button. Play, stop. Rewind, stop. Tuning to the recording should be done with each piece before you start to decipher. Just play along with the bass line long enough to figure out the tonic note, tune it up on the low E string, shut the recorder off, tune up the other five and get to work. If you ever find a blues song to be in D sharp, you are probably listening to a guy who tuned his guitar down a half-step. Sometimes you run into a recording where a capo was used, and this can throw you off until you figure it out. Don't forget, if it's difficut to play, you most likely have the wrong box." The old man looked up to find the boy standing by the open sliding door of the car staring out into the moonlit field the train was passing through.

"Where does this train run, Old Man?"

"Oh, they all go in big loops, you know, Boy. Out and back. Maybe this train will run you down south for awhile, or maybe to Chicago. Then again, it might take you home tomorrow morning. Trust me, Boy. Before long, this train will take you where we need to go."

Somehow the boy found it easy to accept the old man's vague answer. He was happy just to be where he was — with the old man and his guitar.

"Never let too much time slip away, Boy. If you feel like playing the blues one night, then don't sit home! Get behind the feeling and head out to do it! Every blues artist answered that singular personal call, that one feeling to go. Once you step out, then you are on the other side. Expect the turning point. Watch for it to happen. When you see the signposts, Boy, leave everything else behind. Maybe someday you will become the performer and others will slow down your tapes to figure them out. This may be your direction. However, know this: the blues doesn't need another star. The blues just needs you. Let the flame grow. Don't extinguish it with doubt. Sing out loud and clear for the world to hear. Never be a stranger to the blues, Boy. You can always go to it. Reach your centering point and take a look around. Then start to go back up again.

"You know the history of the blues is unwritten, Boy, and will remain so for all time. Blues is just a feeling for life, just a way to state that you are alive. There is no difference between tonight and the night that Charlie Patton walked down to the river with Son House. Get rid of the distance and see it clearly, Boy. We are in the game right now."

The steel wheels of the car turned a regular rhythm under the floorboard as the boy started to play a slow blues on his guitar. The old man joined in, and for hours on end, they played all of the old blues standards and even invented new blues about the night. After a hundred blues, the boy found himself lying on a bed of hay bales in the corner of the boxcar with his guitar across his chest. He could see the moonlit countryside pass through the open door, with the old man sitting against the door frame, playing his guitar.

"Tell me something, Old Man. Don't you ever sleep?"

"Don't have to, Boy. I'm living on blues power."

As the train rolled into the night, the boy fell asleep and the old man played his blues.

20. Blues Forever

unshine broke onto the hay in front of the boy's eyes, bringing him out of sleep. The boy sat up to clear his head as a wave of realization swept over him. He was alone. The boy hung his head and stared at the wooden planks of the floorboard. "So you're gone, Old Man." The boy's voice spilled out into the emptiness of the boxcar. Overcome with grief, the boy sat transfixed, staring out the door opening as the world outside the moving train presented itself in a maze of broken images. The boy quietly stood up and walked in circles to spend his intense feelings.

Now that he was alone it seemed like a dream that he had ever met the old man. The boy played out every day they had spent together in his mind. That strange dawn in the city when he felt a calling to leave and walk the tracks. The night at the campfire when they stayed up all night and the next morning when the old man talked of galaxies, stars and the range of life. The mystery house where equipment was stacked from floor to ceiling. And now, alone.

Looking down, he found a note from the old man stuck in the strings at the top of his guitar. He grabbed the note and held it in the sunlight as he read the message.

"I'm blue, too, Boy. It's not just you that feels this way. I must make my jump off now, and go to teach another. The train will stop in your hometown sometime in the morning, so at least you won't have to jump off while she's moving. That's a blues move I never got to show you. Remember everything I've told you boy. Know I am always with you, and you will never feel alone. I swear on my guitar that I will see you again someday. Play the blues to get it over with, Boy, and get ready for tonight's action."

The boy sat quietly reading the note again and again. He stared at his fingertip and could see the finest particle of dust on his skin. He pretended in his sadness that he could see into the particle where time had stopped, and he could forget his pain.

The train chugged to a slow crawl, and the boy could see the outskirts of his hometown starting to come into view out of the open boxcar door. As the train came to a complete stop, the boy made no movement for the open door, but simply picked up his guitar and started to play. After a few minutes, the train started to move again, and the boy walked over to stand by the door. Once again he watched the city's buildings gradually give way to the countryside. He saw all of the landmarks that went by the morning that he first walked the rails out of his town.

He knew what he had to do. He was counting the minutes until the train would go by the sidetracks that went into the woods where he first met the old man. He laid on his belly and stuck his head out of the car to look down the train to see the approach of his destination. Finally the woods came into view, and the boy knew it was time to make his move. He grabbed his guitar and the cassette deck, and as the train slowed down for the curve, the boy jumped. He landed on his feet, then rolled into the bushes by the roadbed. After dusting himself off and picking up his guitar, he started his walk to the place in the woods by the bridge. Everything was the same as the first time, except the boy heard no sweet music — no wonderful blues. The boy walked slowly up to the spot where he first met the old man and sat down. He put his cassette player to the side and gently strummed his guitar. Not a second was spent considering the mundane affair of numbers and dots. He was beyond that now. He took his feelings out on the guitar and played as never before. Everything the old man had taught him was at his fingertips as he commanded the strings. His feelings overpowered any thought about how he should play. He was too busy riding the edge. Somewhere inside, even beyond his sadness, he knew he was playing the blues!

Suddenly, from out of the corner of his eye, the boy caught a glimpse of movement. Looking up from his guitar he saw a young boy holding a guitar in his hand, shyly looking on with wide eyes. After a long pause, the young stranger asked, "Can you teach me how to play guitar like that?"

Our boy stood up tall, put one foot on the steel rail and took in his own strength. After waiting for a moment, he looked into the youngster's eyes and replied in a low voice, "What do you know about blues history, Boy?"

Appendix

1. Accents

There are three different types of accents that can be placed on a note or chord. An accent is <u>dynamic</u> if it results from greater volume, <u>tonic</u> if it results from higher pitch and <u>agogic</u> if it results from a longer duration of the accented notes.

2. Tempo Marks

Tempo is the rate of speed of the beat. When a piece of music is written down, the writer indicates the tempo with which the piece is to be played by using a series of Italian words, each of which represents an approximate part of the tempo range. Numbers given represent beats per minute.

Largo	Andante	Moderato	Allegretto	Allegro	Vivance	Presto
48	70	90	110	124	158	185
(broad)	(walking)	(moderate)	(rather fast)	(fast)	(faster)	(very fast)

3. Time Signatures

Common meters

Duple (2/2, 2/4, 2/8)
Triple (3/2, 3/4, 3/8)
Quadruple (4/2, 4/4, 4/8)

Compound meters

Compound duple (6/2, 6/4, 6/8)
Compound triple (9/4, 9/8)
Compound quadruple (12/4, 12/8, 12/16)

4. Interval Chart

1 fret	2 fret	3 fret	4 fret	5 fret	6 fret	7 fret	8 fret	9 fret	10 fret	11 fret	12 fret
minor	major	minor	major	perfect	dim.	perfect	minor	major	minor	major	perfect
second	second	third	third	fourth	fifth	fifth	sixth	sixth	seventh	seventh	octave

5. Fundamental Frequency Formula

There are three ways in which the frequency of a string can be varied: length, tension and mass. The fundamental frequency (F) of vibration of a fixed string of length L is given by the following equation where T is the tension in the string and the ML is the mass per unit length of the string.

$$F = \frac{1}{L} \sqrt{\frac{T}{ML}}$$

6. Relative Motion

Two melody lines are said to be: *parallel* if they stay at the same interval away from each other as the line moves, *similar* if they move in the same direction, *contrary* if they are moving away from each other in opposite directions, and *oblique* if one part remains at the same pitch.

7. Other Books and Blues Recordings

The first thing I'll tell you is to go to the largest library around where you live and look up Blues in the card catalog. You might be surprised at what is there. Large universities usually have special music libraries, or at least a section for music in the main library. Here you will find a wealth of books about all kinds of music including blues, jazz and rock. Just walk up and down by the shelves and check it out. There are numerous music encyclopedias and dictionaries to be found in these libraries, and some are available in condensed form over the counter in book stores. My favorite is the Harvard Brief Dictionary of Music, a little gold mine of a music book.

The Story of the Blues by Paul Oliver is without a doubt the most definitive blues history book written to date. A joy to read and wonderfully illustrated with hundreds of old pictures of performers and the world of the blues, this is the book you want if you are interested in the history of the blues. Thank you, Paul Oliver.

The Rolling Stone Illustrated History of Rock and Roll picks up in the early fifties where The Story of the Blues leaves off. Easily available on the open market, this massive 72-chapter work gives you the whole picture by presenting you with topic articles written by a large variety of artists and writers.

Feel Like Going Home: Portraits in Blues and Rock and Roll by Peter Guralnick is an interesting, freely written book that will give you great insights into the lives of a number of blues artists.

The old man already talked about "Hit The Bins," so I'll let that be. Crescendo Records has a great series of blues records in twelve volumes, all tied together by a book called The Legacy of the Blues by Samuel Charters. Their address is: 9165 Sunset Boulevard, Los Angeles, CA 90069

Yazoo Records, 245 Waverly Place, New York, NY 10014, has a great mail order catalog for old blues records and other interesting blues products like a baseball card type series called "Heroes of the Blues" illustrated by R. Crumb.

Rounder Records, 186 Willow Avenue, Somerville, MA 02144, is a small record company that has a catalog of blues artists.

Guitar Player International, 20605 Lazeneo, Cupertino, CA, has published a huge body of work relating to the guitar. They have a great line of guitar related books, and also publish *Guitar Player Magazine* which interviews a different professional each month.

Great visions. That's what it takes to truly understand the guitar, Boy. And that is exactly what you are in for when you hear the lowdown on these *accelerated learning sound cassettes.* They were created to complement your knowledge gained from this book and were recorded with the same full tilt attitude that you have found in its pages. As soon as you press the play button on your cassette player, you better take two steps back, and get your guitar in tune and get ready to get intense. Because, when it comes to teaching guitar, I DON'T WASTE TIME. Everything is qued up tight and perfectly in tune with the A 440 tuning fork which I sound for you several times during the course of the tapes, just to keep you in tune with the jive, Boy. Hey, I don't expect you to keep up with me the first time through, that's why they design quick rewind buttons into those things. And I fully expect you to use it in order to pick up on every little gem that you hear. You've gotta hear to know what I'm talking about.

The Fifty Blues Moves Cassette

This one hour tape was created to make the fifty blues moves found in chapter sixteen of this book come alive with sound. Each passage is given strict individual attention including a verbal rundown spotlighting how the move works, along with precise recordings of each move exactly as it is transcribed. Several of the riffs are presented more than once in order to demonstrate loose interpretations or special effects. Everything you see in chapter sixteen, you will hear on this tape.

The Old Man Talks and Plays

The Old Man takes over for one hour playing out the secrets only he knows. First he will tell you the truth, then he will play it straight on his guitar to prove his point. The spectrum of topics that you read about in the book will come to life on the master's guitar. Tricks of the trade, gritty rhythms, overall guitar scales, chord changes, lead guitar insights, playing the blues fast and easy — it is all spelled out for you step-by-step. Along with the tape comes a technical guidebook layed out in sections called Windows to the Blues which provide you with all of the transcriptions and diagrams referred to on the tape. It all adds up to this — when you work with him "one-on-one", you learn fast.

Pocket Full of Blues

Understand what this tape is right off the bat. You get four blues tunes on side one in the key of E, and four more on side two in the key of A. All songs are recorded so you can play along with the old man as if he were standing next to you down at the corner juke BACKING YOU UP!!! That's right — you get the skeleton of the blues form played eight different ways ready for you to fill up the cup again and again however you want. The first time through the structure the old man takes the lead, but after that, he nails down the rhythm to give you complete freedom to improvise, sing, blow the harp or scream the blues until all is well. Key tuning fork soundings open each tune — then you're off — not a spoken word on the tape. Most are twelve bar, but you get a great variety of tempo, rhythm, a solo acoustic number, an eight bar blues and a turnaround. The emphasis is definitely on straight out rocking. A guidebook is provided to spell out the lowdown on Bar/Chord/Key/Tempo. Pop this cassette into your pocket and head out for the day. Say, isn't that the old man walking toward the corner with his electric guitar case?

Helpful Fretboard Dots

See the fretboard *come alive with the right notes* with the aid of these custom designed guitar fretboard dots. Use these adhesive dots to "set up" any musical scale on any part of the board. Many and varied in their design, these dots will quickly and easily reveal the workings of the fretboard. Chord inversion, parallel boxes, lowered degrees, *blues, major or minor scales,* set up whatever you want to learn.

Thoughtfully designed to accommodate the guitarist, Helpful Fretboard Dots were printed in many useful sets of *numbers and letter name notes* in both squares and circles, black and white, to identify each degree of any desired scale. Along with these dots, you also get the *Symbols to Understand:* five token symbols (star, half moon, etc.) printed in red to highlight any chosen note. Also included are 20 fretboard diagrams to aid in set up, 13 major and blues scale fingerings on six line guitar staff, chord and scale charts, and complete set up directions for the LEAD ROCK GUITARIST. Confidence, speed and fretboard knowledge can all be yours with Helpful Fretboard Dots.

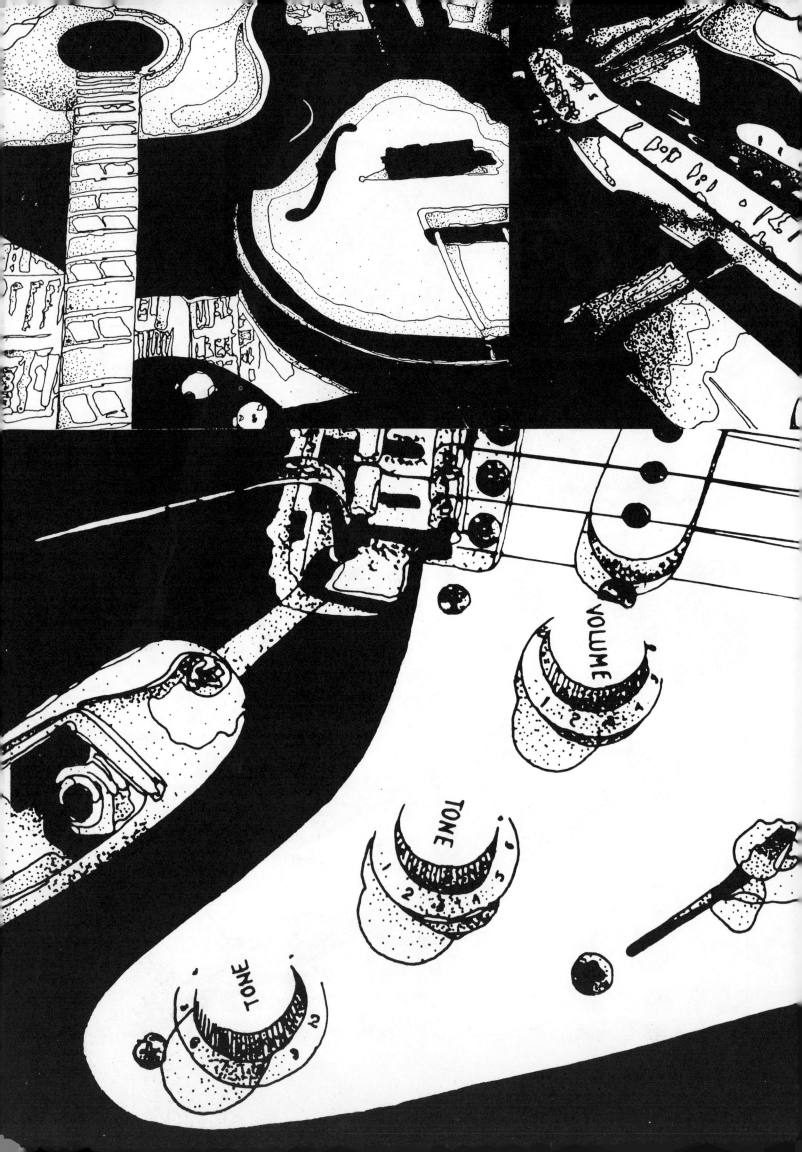